THE
LITTLE
BOOK
OF
WELSH
CULTURE

THE
LITTLE
BOOK
OF
WELSH
CULTURE

MARK REES

The
History
Press

First published 2016

The History Press
The Mill, Brimscombe Port
Stroud, Gloucestershire, GL5 2QG
www.thehistorypress.co.uk

British Library Cataloguing in Publication Data.
A catalogue record for this book is available from the British Library.

ISBN 978 0 7509 6774 7

Typesetting and origination by The History Press
Printed and bound in Great Britain by TJ International Ltd. Padstow

Front cover image: Eisteddfod Tent by Peter Broster
(creativecommons.org/licenses/by/2.0/legalcode)

CONTENTS

ABOUT THE AUTHOR

Mark Rees was born and raised in Port Talbot and educated through the medium of Welsh. He has been working in the media in Wales for over a decade as the arts supplement editor and reviewer for the *South Wales Evening Post*, the What's On editor for *Swansea Life* and *Cowbridge Life* magazines, and as a regular contributor to the *Carmarthen Journal* and *Llanelli Star*. He has hosted arts-based radio shows and documentaries and is a nominator for the Wales Theatre Awards.

'Mark is one of the very few journalists whose enthusiasm and support for the arts and entertainment in Wales transcends his day job and is clearly in his bones.'

Michael Smith, *Arts Scene in Wales* editor
and Wales Theatre Awards director

'With his extensive knowledge and passion, Mark is most definitely an ambassador for the arts in Wales.'

Nia Jones, Wales Millennium Centre marketing manager

'Mark's inquisitive mind and apposite comments are hugely important and are a benchmark for our own efforts in maintaining a healthy and vibrant cultural environment.'

Paul Hopkins, Swansea Grand Theatre programme,
marketing and development manager

'It seems a shame that Mark has written this book. Had anybody else been the author, he would have featured in it extensively himself.'

Owen Staton, actor and Welsh storyteller

ACKNOWLEDGEMENTS

First and foremost, a huge diolch o galon to my family for their unwavering support, and apologies for any prolonged absences and unanswered messages during the months spent researching and writing this book. To my editors past and present – Wyn Jenkins, Peter Slee and Jonathan Roberts – for not only allowing me to write about my passion, but for actually paying me for the privilege as well. And to Nicola Guy and everyone at The History Press for commissioning the book that you now hold in your hands.

A little book of Welsh culture would not have been possible without the backing of the *South Wales Evening Post*, and everyone working in the arts in Wales who very kindly gave up their time to assist with my requests for images and information, in particular: Paul Hopkins and all at Swansea Grand Theatre; Sara Jones and all at BBC Cymru Wales; Nia Jones and all at the Wales Millennium Centre; Branwen Jones and all at the Welsh National Opera; Catrin Rogers and all at the National Theatre Wales; Jo Furber and all at the Dylan Thomas Centre; Adrian Metcalfe and all at the Lighthouse Theatre Company; Jeff Towns, the world's leading authority on all things Dylan Thomas; and Mal Pope, an absolute gentleman and the finest barista this side of Brazil.

I would also like to express my gratitude to archivist extraordinaire Pat Jones, whose knowledge knows no bounds; Owen Staton, the king of Welsh storytelling; Mike Smith, a relentless crusader for the arts and a friendly face at the opera; Chris Carra and Fifty One Productions, for joining me on my first attempt to unpack Wales on film; and to Jean and Lindsay for keeping me in hot meals and football tickets throughout the season.

INTRODUCTION

Welsh academic and novelist Raymond Williams described the word culture in his *Keywords: A Vocabulary of Culture and Society* (1976) as 'one of the two or three most complicated words in the English language' and, having researched its meaning ahead of writing this book, I find it hard to disagree.

Fortunately, for the purposes of *The Little Book of Welsh Culture*, I haven't had to analyse the word's early origins or historical evolution as Williams did, but merely to use it in its modern-day context, namely as a word to describe the way of life for a group of people and, more predominantly, the arts.

To reflect this, this book has been divided into seven chapters.

The first is an overview of all the core cultural features that make Wales the great country that it is, many of which reoccur throughout the book – the language, the symbols, the festivals and the traditions.

The remaining chapters take a chronological journey through the arts themselves, from the ancient bards to the visionary landscape painters, and the opera house-filling superstars to the Academy Award-winning actors.

By its very nature, this 'little book' is intended as a snappy overview of Welsh culture and doesn't pretend to be a comprehensive guide, but I have endeavoured to squeeze as many facts and details into this small volume as I possibly can.

I hope you enjoy this book and, if nothing else, I hope that it inspires you to investigate some of the subjects further – to visit a gallery, to download a song, to read a book, or maybe even learn a few words of yr iaith Gymraeg.

Mark Rees, 2016

1

THE CULTURE OF WALES

To be born in Wales,
Not with a silver spoon in your mouth,
But, with music in your blood
And with poetry in your soul,
Is a privilege indeed.

Brian Harris, *In Passing* (1967)

THE WELSH LANGUAGE

From the early verses of the sixth-century bards to the rousing national anthem and the annual National Eisteddfod, arguably the single most influential factor in the history of Welsh culture is the Welsh language – yr iaith Gymraeg.

For those who can speak it, it is a constant source of pride and inspiration, and for those who can't, they need look no further than the bilingual street signs or tune in to a Welsh-language radio station for a taste of its lyricism.

The oldest language in Britain, it is thought to have emerged, in its most primitive form, in the middle of the sixth century, evolving from Common Brittonic, the Celtic language which was spoken across what is now Wales, England and southern Scotland.

English is now the predominant language in Wales, with the United Kingdom Census 2011 revealing that only 19 per cent of the population can speak their native tongue. But while it is assumed that there are no monoglot Welsh-speakers remaining, there are still many for whom Welsh is their first language, predominantly in west and north-west Wales.

The reasons for the decline have been attributed to several factors, from mass immigration during the Industrial Revolution to, more recently, English being the global language of choice in the Internet age, but there was also systematic suppression, with the most infamous example being The Welsh Not.

A punishment introduced for schoolchildren in the late nineteenth century, pupils caught speaking their own language would have a wooden board hung over their neck inscribed with the initials WN. The Not would be passed on to the next child who transgressed, with the unfortunate bearer at the end of the day being severely caned for their heinous crime.

In modern-day Wales the opposite is now true, and since 2000 the teaching of the Welsh language has been made compulsory in all schools.

In 2011, following a unanimous vote by the National Assembly for Wales, royal approval was given to the *Welsh Language (Wales) Measure* which conferred official status on the language, and saw the appointment of a Welsh Language Commissioner to ensure that anyone wishing to live their life solely through the medium of Welsh should be treated no differently to anyone using the English language in Wales.

SYMBOLS OF WALES

The Welsh flag: Wales is the only home country not represented in the Union Jack, the national flag of the United Kingdom which combines aspects from the crosses of England's St George, Scotland's St Andrew, and Ireland's St Patrick.

Fortunately, in the Red Dragon (Y Ddraig Goch) it has a much more visually appealing flag of its own, displaying the iconic image of a mythological fire-breathing creature standing firmly on the green, green grass of home with a claw raised defiantly to the white sky.

The Welsh dragon's origins are steeped in myth and folklore, and can be traced back to the ninth-century *Historia Brittonum* in which a red dragon and a white dragon are fighting underground. An analogy for the native Britons fighting the invading Saxons, the tale was expanded upon in the twelfth century by Geoffrey of Monmouth in his *Historia Regum Britanniae* (*History of the Kings of Britain*), and the Mabinogion prose tale *Lludd and Llefelys*.

It is thought that King Arthur might have brandished a dragon on his standard, as did Cadwaladr, a Middle Age king of Gwynedd, and its use could possibly be traced back to an emblem used by the Roman military.

Owain Glyndŵr, the last native Welshman to hold the title Prince of Wales and an enduring symbol of Welsh nationalism, brandished a golden dragon (Y Ddraig Aur) while rebelling against the English.

In the fifteenth century, the House of Tudor added their green and white livery to the Red Dragon after Henry Tudor, of Welsh ancestry, carried the flag into St Paul's Cathedral as he took the English throne from Richard III after the Battle of Bosworth.

In 1807, the Red Dragon was set to a green base and became the Royal Badge of Wales, and formed the basis for the current incarnation of the flag, which was given official status by the government in 1959.

St David's flag: The flag of St David, a yellow cross on a black background, is considered to be the unofficial second flag of Wales. Deriving its colours from the diocese of St David's coat of arms, it can be seen across Wales on St David's Day, and has been used as a symbol of nationalism, by the 38th (Welsh) Infantry Division during the Second World War, on the badge of Cardiff City Football Club, and even by a group of devout Christians who have called for it to replace the official flag, claiming that the Red Dragon represents the Devil himself.

Prince of Wales' Feathers: The heraldic badge of the Prince of Wales is often used to symbolise Wales, most prominently on the jerseys of the

Illustration of a woman in traditional Welsh dress
from George Borrow's *Wild Wales*, 1907.

Welsh rugby union players and by members of the military. Its design –
three ostrich feathers held inside a golden crown above the slogan
Ich dien ('I serve' in German) – can be traced back to the fourteenth
century.

The national dress: In the late eighteenth century, the practical clothing
worn by rural Welsh women caught the imaginations of tourists and
printmakers alike, and the concept of a traditional Welsh costume
was born.

The outfit survives to this day, and can regularly be seen at patriotic
events such as eisteddfodau, St David's Day school celebrations, and at
many tourist destinations – if only to appease modern-day sightseers.

Regional variations aside, it typically consists of a bedgown and skirt,
both with strong colours and usually a striped design, a distinctive
shawl made from Welsh wool, a cape with a large hood, and its most
distinctive feature, a tall, rigid hat which is worn on top of a cap or
handkerchief.

Notable for her efforts in popularising the look is Augusta Hall,
Baroness Llanover, a Welsh arts enthusiast who wrote the 1834
National Eisteddfod prize-winning essay 'The Advantages resulting
from the Preservation of the Welsh language and National Costume
of Wales'.

The leek, the national emblem of Wales: Emblazoned on the Welsh pound coin and worn with pride on St David's Day, the exact details of how the green and white – and somewhat pungent – leek became the national emblem for Wales are now lost to time, but it has been suggested that its origins date back to the times of the Druids, who believed that the vegetable held magical healing properties.

There are early references to the leek in the colour scheme of the outfits of fourteenth-century archers, and guards working during the Tudor dynasty are known to have worn them on St David's Day.

In William Shakespeare's play *Henry V*, dated around 1599, King Henry V describes the custom as an ancient tradition and tells Captain Fluellen that he is wearing one 'for I am Welsh, you know, good countryman'.

In a story recorded in the seventeenth century by English poet Michael Drayton, it was claimed that St David himself instructed his soldiers to wear leeks in their hats as they battled the Saxons, which wouldn't have been hard to come by as the battle took place in a field of leeks.

The daffodil, the national flower of Wales: As with the leek, the daffodil is proudly displayed every St David's Day, pinned on clothing or even, during rugby matches, in the form of a head-covering hat.

A debate broke out in the nineteenth century in which it was argued that the daffodil was actually the true emblem of Wales, and that the less aromatic leek had been mistakenly chosen due to the similarity of their Welsh names: cennin for leek, and cenhinen Bedr (Peter's leek) for daffodil.

Despite the leek emerging victorious, the daffodil found favour with many, including Welsh Prime Minister David Lloyd George, and established itself as an alternative, if not a replacement.

THE PATRON SAINT OF WALES

St David's Day (Dydd Gŵyl Dewi Sant), 1 March: Wales' Patron Saint's Day is a time of national celebration, marked by parades, public events and, particularly in schools, eisteddfodau, and the wearing of national symbols and traditional dress.

Held annually since the eighteenth century on what is thought to have been the day of his death, St David was a deeply spiritual man who promoted a simple life of piety and abstinence, which included no meat and no alcohol, and is said to have lived for 100 years.

Several miracles were attributed to the sixth-century bishop, the most well known of which relates to a time when the ground rose from beneath his feet while preaching in Llanddewi Brefi, allowing the word of God to be seen and heard far and wide, as a white dove symbolically settled on his shoulder, establishing itself as the saint's emblem.

St David's Day, which many in Wales have petitioned to be made an official bank holiday, is celebrated around the world wherever the Welsh can be found. The largest North American event is the St David's Day Festival in Los Angeles, while Disneyland Paris marks the occasion with a St David's Welsh Festival weekend, during which Mickey and friends host concerts in Welsh costume, and add a Welsh-theme to the daily parade and fireworks displays.

THE PATRON SAINT OF LOVERS

St Dwynwen's Day (Dydd Santes Dwynwen), 25 January: While not as prevalent in Wales as St Valentine's Day, the increasingly popular Dydd Santes Dwynwen is celebrated annually in much the same way, with the giving of romantic cards and flowers, and the added Welsh spin of love spoons.

Named after the fifth-century saint of love, who forsook love for herself in order to bring it to others, legend has it that Dwynwen fell in love with the unattainable suitor Maelon Dafodrill, and prayed to have all thoughts of her beloved removed.

Answering her plea, an angel arrived with a potion that not only erased Dafodrill from her memory, but froze him into a block of ice. When God granted Dwynwen three wishes, her first was to thaw her former sweetheart from his icy prison, the second was to ask God to take care of all true lovers, and the third was that she would remain unmarried for the rest of her life.

The reason for the final wish was to allow her to devote her life to God's service, taking the nun's habit in Anglesey where the remains of her church can be seen on the island of Llanddwyn.

Love Spoons: Dating back to at least the seventeenth century, the handmade Welsh love spoon is a time-honoured tradition that remains popular in the craft and gift shops of Wales today.

While not originally unique to Wales, with several other European countries producing love spoons of their own, while the tradition has all but died out elsewhere, it has flourished and taken on a distinctly Welsh character in the passing centuries.

As the name would suggest, their original purpose was purely romantic and they were gifted as a symbol of commitment, but while the materials needed to create the spoons would have been readily available, the real skill lay in the hands of the crafts people who transformed a simple piece of timber into a magical keepsake.

The oldest surviving example from 1667 can be seen on display at Cardiff's St Fagans National History Museum.

NADOLIG LLAWEN (MERRY CHRISTMAS)

Christmas in Wales is the largest celebration of the year, a time of goodwill when workers down tools to exchange presents, and to overindulge in food and drink, with their nearest and dearest.

But it wasn't always this way. Traditionally, **New Year's Eve** was seen as the highlight of the Christmastime calendar, with Christmas Day itself considered to be more of a religious occasion.

On **Christmas Eve,** it was customary to decorate the house with evergreens in preparation for the big day, with holly symbolising eternal life, and mistletoe to ward off evil. There'd be singing and dancing until late into the night, and in some areas they'd make cyflaith (taffy) before the early morning pilgrimage to church.

Plygain (matins) singing would traditionally take place between 3 a.m. and 6 a.m., in which the men, and later the women when allowed to join in, would sing carols until daybreak. As regular services were rarely held in the dark, an important feature of the festival was the use of plygain candles, with each parishioner bringing their own candle to spectacularly illuminate the church.

On **Gŵyl San Steffan (St Stephen's Day/Boxing Day)**, regional customs in honour of the Christian martyr included the bloodletting of livestock – believed to be for their own benefit – and the painful practice of holming, in which unfortunate individuals – usually female servants, or the last person to rise – were lashed on the arms and legs with branches of holly.

MARI LWYD

One of the more peculiar Welsh Christmastime folk traditions is the Mari Lwyd, a wassailing custom that would usually take place on New Year's Eve.

A gang of men would go from home to home brandishing the Mari Lwyd, a hooded animal much like a hobby horse, which was assembled by attaching the skull of a horse, adorned with ribbons and bells and complete with moveable jaw, to the end of a pole held upright by a carrier concealed under a sheet.

The group, directed by a leader decked out in his Sunday best and accompanied by musicians and others dressed as characters such as Punch and Siwan (Judy), would attempt to gain entry to the home through the use of pwngco – a playful battle of song, in which a verse is sung by the visitors, and the occupiers attempt to repel them with a verse of their own.

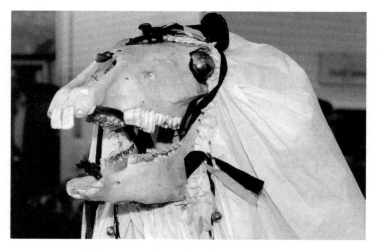

The Mari Lwyd. (*South Wales Evening Post*)

If successful, the Mari Lwyd would cause mischief in the house, chasing the girls and scaring the children, while the leader would do his best – or at least pretend – to keep it under control until they received their reward of food and drink.

While the tradition of disturbing neighbours in the early hours of the morning has been consigned to the past, there are still areas of Wales where the Mari Lwyd is practiced in a more respectable form, most notably in the village of Llangynwyd, just south of Maesteg, where a visit to the Old House Inn on New Year's Eve will still bring you face to face with a horse's skull.

SEASONAL FESTIVALS

New Year's Day (Dydd Calan), 1 January: Preceded by much merriment during New Year's Eve (Nos Galan), it was traditional for children to go door-to-door before noon on New Year's Day with good tidings and song while brandishing a skewered apple decorated with evergreen in return for gifts of calennig – usually money or food.

Twelfth Night (Nos Ystwyll), 5 January: Along with the removal of Christmas decorations, which were buried with seeds in the hope of a good spring, the unusual custom of Hunting the Wren occurred on Twelfth Night. The miniscule bird was hunted and caged, before being paraded around the houses where payments were given in return for a glimpse of the feathered prisoner.

Feast of the Epiphany (Ystwyll), 6 January: Glamorganshire had its own unique way of marking God's manifestation as a human by hiding a ring inside a loaf of bread or cake and breaking it into three pieces – one for Christ, one for the Virgin Mary, and one for the Three Wise Men. The lucky ring-finder would be nominated king or queen for the day.

Mary's Festival of the Candles (Gŵyl Fair y Canhwyllau), 2 February: The pagan Festival of the Candles, which became the Welsh Candlemas when Mary's name was added to the title, was a time when those who had been allowed to work by candlelight during the dark winter months handed back their candles. Customs included divination and the wishing for an abundant year.

Shrove Tuesday (Dydd Mawrth Ynyd): The tradition of feasting on the day before Lent saw the last of the supplies used up to make crempogs (pancakes), with surplus food given away to poorer members of the communities. But it was accompanied by a rather unpleasant custom for the supplier of its main ingredient: any hen which failed to lay its eggs before noon was buried up to its neck in the ground while blindfolded participants took it in turns to try smacking it with a stick. The first to succeed would claim the hen as their own – to be eaten the next day.

Easter (Pasg): In keeping with the resurrection theme, Sul y Blodau (Sunday of the Flowers) on Palm Sunday was a time for out with the old, in with the new – for the living as well as the dead. New clothes would be worn, and graves would be given a makeover, cleaned and decorated with flowers. Dydd Gwener y Groglith (Good Friday) was seen as a day of rest, and the streets would be deserted but for those making their way barefoot to church out of respect for Christ's resting place beneath their feet. On Llun y Pasg (Easter Monday), crowds would gather on the highest mountain points to witness the sunrise, which symbolised Christ rising from the grave.

May Day (Calan Mai), 1 May: A celebration of love and rebirth when bonfires are lit to herald the arrival of summer. Traditions included divinations, dawnsio haf (summer dancing), carolau haf (summer carols), brightening up homes with flowers, and the appointment of a May King and Queen.

Calan Awst (Lammas Day), first day of August: The Welsh equivalent of the Gaelic festival Lughnasadh was a time for celebrating the year's first harvest with drink, dance and song.

Halloween (Nos Galan Gaeaf), 31 October: Nos Galan Gaeaf is a time when spirits roam the land, haunting crossroads and lurking in graveyards. Revellers would dance around bonfires and place a stone bearing their name into the flames, before hurrying home to avoid any of the apparitions that might be abroad – in particular, Yr Hwch Ddu Gwta (The Tailless Black Sow), and the ladi wen (lady in white). If anyone found their stone to be missing the next morning on Calan Gaeaf – the first day of winter – it was considered to be an ominous prophesy of impending death in the coming year.

THE NATIONAL EISTEDDFOD

The most important dates in the Welsh-speaking cultural calendar are reserved for the eisteddfodau (the plural of eisteddfod) – a competitive festival of the arts which can be traced back to the twelfth century and which thrives today thanks to a romanticised revival in the eighteenth century.

Said to be the largest festival of competitive music and poetry in Europe, the name derives from a combination of the Welsh words eistedd (sit) and bod (to be). The nearest English translation is the word session.

The first known eisteddfod took place during the Christmas period of 1176 at Cardigan Castle, the home of Rhys ap Gruffydd, the Lord Rhys, where the custom of awarding a chair for the best poem began. The first large-scale gathering was in Carmarthen in 1451, while the first use of the word eisteddfod to describe the festival dates from Caerwys in 1523.

The fortunes of the eisteddfod mirrored those of the professional barding tradition in Wales which declined in the sixteenth century, and early attempts to revive the festival in the eighteenth century amounted to little more than a handful of poets gathered in a tavern. The turning point came when Thomas Jones, an exciseman from Corwen, approached the London-based Welsh literary and cultural Gwyneddigion Society in 1789, which set in motion the modern concepts of professionalism, forward planning, and an open door to the public.

Ray Gravell lifting the ceremonial sword ahead of the Swansea National Eisteddfod, 2006. (*South Wales Evening Post* / Adrian White)

In 1792, Iolo Morganwg – the bardic name of Edward Williams (1747–1826) from Pen-onn – established what has become an integral part of the eisteddfod when the Gorsedd Beirdd Ynys Prydain (Gorsedd of the Bards of the Isle of Britain) first met in London's Primrose Hill.

One of Wales's most important, if notorious, cultural figures, Williams was an expert antiquarian and an authority on medieval literature, but his reputation was tarnished when it was discovered that – for all his good intentions – he was also a forger who fabricated much of his work to serve his own ends of reviving Welsh culture by any means necessary.

As such, many of the ancient druidic rituals and ceremonies performed by the Gorsedd at eisteddfodau today might be considered to be time-honoured traditions in the sense that they date back hundreds of years, but not thousands of years as originally claimed.

Spurred on by the indignity of the Treachery of the Blue Books in 1847, an English-commissioned report which branded the Welsh working class as 'ignorant, lazy and immoral' due to their language and religious beliefs, the search for a Welsh cultural renaissance gained new impetus, and following 'the great Llangollen Eisteddfod of 1858', the National Eisteddfod Council, who combined with the governing Gorsedd, was established.

In 1860, The Eisteddfod was born in Denbigh, and a year later the first National Eisteddfod of Wales was held in Aberdare, and continues annually to this day on the first week of August, alternating its location between North and South Wales.

A family friendly festival which offers the best of Welsh culture, from traditional choral singing to modern-day hip hop dancing, the heart of the eisteddfod is the Maes (field or area), populated by stall holders offering everything from local food to contemporary art and where over 6,000 participants read, sing and perform entirely in the Welsh-language in the Pafiliwn (Pavilion).

Some of the Gorsedd's druidic ceremonies are also held in the Pafiliwn as well as at their Gorsedd stones (a stone circle, either permanent or, since 2005, temporary), while new members are welcomed with a lively procession through the Maes. The Crowning of the Bard (Coroni'r Bardd) ceremony usually takes place on the Monday, and the Chairing of the Bard (Cadeirio'r Bardd) on the Friday.

While the National Eisteddfod might be a celebration of the Welsh language, it can still be enjoyed by non-Welsh speakers, who can learn some of the language in a programme for beginners. In an effort to broaden the festival's appeal, an 'open festival plan' has been proposed for future events in which the host location's existing buildings would be used instead of the traditional Maes.

URDD NATIONAL EISTEDDFOD

In much the same way as the National Eisteddfod, the Urdd National Eisteddfod (Eisteddfod Genedlaethol yr Urdd) is an annual cultural competition, but aimed at young people aged 7 to 24.

Thought to be Europe's largest youth festival, it takes place during the May half-term, and also alternates from North to South Wales, with every fourth year taking place in Cardiff Bay's Wales Millennium Centre.

The week-long televised festival provides a unique platform for young artists to hone their skills, and its competitions, which include Cân Actol (singing and acting) and Cerdd Dant (traditional string music), have been credited with helping to launch the careers of many an established artist.

The organisers Urdd Gobaith Cymru (the Welsh League of Hope or the Welsh League of Youth) were established in 1922 by Sir Ifan ab Owen Edwards, the son of Sir Owen Morgan Edwards, and the youth movement has endeared itself to generations of Welsh-language schoolchildren with its instantly recognisable logo and mascot Mistar Urdd (Mr Urdd) and his infectious theme song 'Hei, Mistar Urdd yn dy goch gwyn a gwyrdd' (Hey, Mr Urdd in your red, white and green).

THE INTERNATIONAL EISTEDDFOD

The International Eisteddfod – not to be confused with the National Eisteddfod – is an annual eisteddfod with a global outlook which takes place in Llangollen, Denbighshire, for six days every July.

Welcoming some of the most accomplished artists from around the world, it promotes a message of peace and internationalism as the cultures of around fifty different nations take to the stage and, in one of the festival's highlights, to the streets of the town for a colourful parade.

The daily competitions, which once saw a young Luciano Pavarotti compete on Welsh soil, are followed by evening concerts that allow some of the competitors to perform alongside established professionals.

EISTEDDFODAU AROUND THE WORLD

Eisteddfodau are not limited to Wales, or even to the Welsh language, and variations can be found in places like Jersey and Bristol, and even the National Eisteddfod itself has occasionally taken place in England.

Further afield, the concept of the eisteddfod has been adopted in Australia, and found a natural home-from-home in Argentina following the 1865 Welsh settlement in Patagonia, where several bilingual eisteddfodau – Spanish and Welsh – take place annually.

A network of Welsh-American societies stage eisteddfodau across North America, with singing and recitation competitions taking place during the Welsh North American Society's wonderfully diverse North American Festival of Wales and the Malad Valley Welsh Festival in Idaho.

The Welsh Society of Philadelphia's Cynonfardd Eisteddfod, held annually in Edwardsville, Pennsylvania, is thought to be the oldest continuous eisteddfod after the National Eisteddfod, having been established by Dr Thomas C. Edwards in 1889 following the settlement of Welsh coal miners.

CULTURAL MUST-SEES

Hay Festival (end of May): Described by former American president Bill Clinton as 'the Woodstock of the mind', the inspirational Hay Festival is Wales' leading literature and arts festival.

Set in Hay-on-Wye, the Welsh 'town of books' at the peak of the Brecon Beacons National Park, it gathers together some of the world's greatest thinkers – including writers, scientists, environmentalists, filmmakers and politicians – for eleven days of thought-provoking discussion, the exchange of ideas, and out-and-out entertainment from comedians and musicians.

Founded in 1987 by the father and son team of Norman Florence and festival director Peter Florence, it is said to have begun life around a kitchen table, funded by the winnings of a poker game.

The festival has since expanded to include the Hay Fever festival for children, along with a festive three-day Winter Weekend in the heart of the town at Christmas, and international sister festivals in five different continents.

Wakestock Gŵyl y Môr/Festival of the Sea (July): Described as Europe's largest wakeboard music festival, Wakestock on the Llŷn Peninsula combines the popular water sport with contemporary music to the backdrop of sand, sea and (occasionally) sun. Set on the North Wales coastline, the festival for the young – and the young at heart – began life in Abersoch in 2000, and now encompasses additional locations in Penrhos and Pwllheli.

Green Man Festival (August): What began in 2003 as a small gathering in the Brecon Beacons has snowballed into Wales' coolest music festival, while remaining true to its non-corporate roots by having no sponsors or advertising – it simply lets the music do the talking. The four-day festival's eclectic line-up welcomes some of the hottest up-and-coming bands alongside established acts to Wales, with family friendly distractions and platforms for spoken word, comedy, literature and cinema.

Brecon Jazz Festival (August): The market town of Brecon becomes Wales' jazz heartland every August when some of the best artists from around the world head to the hills for three days of live music. Founded by jazz journalist, musician, promoter and all-round jazz enthusiast Jed Williams in 1984, the festival now takes place alongside the Brecon Fringe Festival, which brings even more music to the surrounding pubs and clubs.

Festival N°6 (September): Wonderfully eccentric and intrinsically Welsh at heart, if not necessarily in appearance, the coastal tourist village of Portmeirion – an Italian-inspired hamlet designed and built by Sir Clough Williams-Ellis – plays host to a the three-day festival that embraces all styles of music alongside comedy, talks and poetry. Founded in 2012, it derives its name from the cult TV series *The Prisoner*, which popularised the area on the small screen in the 1960s.

The Good Life Experience (September): Flintshire's The Good Life Experience was established by Cerys Matthews and Charlie and Caroline Gladstone in 2014 to – as the name suggests – provide a festival experience that promotes a simpler way of life. Set on the Hawarden Estate, the all-ages gathering encourages discovery and wellbeing through music, food, the arts, and the great outdoors, with events ranging from abseiling to Tai Chi.

Sŵn Festival (October): Inspired by America's South By South West (SXSW) festival, Cardiff-born Radio 1 DJ Huw Stephens and Welsh Music Prize co-founder John Rostron's lively multi-venue music festival sees around 200 artists performing across the capital. Launched in 2007, the annual event is a winner of the Best Small Festival award at the NME Awards.

Dylan Thomas Festival (October): Spanning the dates of Dylan Thomas' birth (27 October) and death (9 November), Swansea's Dylan Thomas Centre celebrates the life of their namesake with two weeks of inventive literary events that include talks, book launches and arts and crafts.

Fans of the poet will find no shortage of other events taking place in his honour throughout the year, including the Do Not Go Gentle Festival, a three-day arts festival with a line-up of acts that 'Dylan might have liked' which takes place earlier in October around the bard's birthplace in Uplands, and the annual Laugharne Weekend, a compact and intimate literary and arts festival set in the Carmarthenshire town. The annual Dylan Day is a global event held on 14 May – the date *Under Milk Wood* was first read on stage in New York in 1953.

Folk music and dancing: Folk dancing can be seen on the streets of Cardiff during Gŵyl Ifan, with dancers from across Europe joining those in Wales for three days of traditional dance to mark midsummer in June, while the Tredegar House Folk Festival, set in a seventeenth-century National Trust property in Newport, aims to educate as well as entertain. Established *gŵyl werin* (folk festivals) can be found in Fishguard and Gower, while Cwlwm Celtaidd in Porthcawl welcomes artists from Ireland, Scotland, Isle of Man, Cornwall and Brittany for a Celtic gathering of song and dance.

CLASSICAL MUSIC FESTIVALS

St Davids Cathedral Festival (May): St Davids' stunning cathedral hosts an annual ten-day classical music festival during the spring bank holiday, with evening concerts from leading musicians and daytime recitals for emerging talent.

Vale of Glamorgan Festival (May): In 1992, the Vale of Glamorgan Festival announced that it would become a festival for living composers only, setting itself apart from those who perform mainly the classical repertoire and establishing itself as a haven for contemporary music. Founded by composer John Metcalf in 1969, it welcomes a diverse range of global musicians to venues across Cardiff and the Vale of Glamorgan.

Gregynog Festival (June): Revived in 1988, having been originally launched by Welsh arts patrons Gwendoline and Margaret Davies in 1933, the 'oldest extant classical music festival in Wales' at Gregynog Hall, Tregynon, embraces the arts as a whole and has a reputation for attracting some of the biggest names in classical music.

BBC Cardiff Singer of the World Competition (June): Launched in 1983 to coincide with the opening of Cardiff's St David's Hall, the bi-annual singing competition has given an international platform to some of opera's emerging stars, with Wales' Bryn Terfel winning the inaugural Lieder Prize (now the Song Prize) in 1989. Broadcast around the world on radio, televisions and online, the competition, which has Dame Kiri Te Kanawa as its patron, is judged by a selection of industry specialists, while the Dame Joan Sutherland Audience Prize is decided by a public vote.

The Gower Festival (July): Combining natural and musical beauty, the churches of the Gower Peninsula throw open their doors to local and touring musicians for two weeks every summer. The festival can trace its origins back to 1976, when the concept was adapted following a series of thirty-one concerts performed by a student orchestra led by cellist Jonathan Beecher.

The Welsh Proms (July): Founded by artistic director Owain Arwel Hughes in 1986, Wales' National Classical Music Festival offers orchestral favourites alongside contemporary fringe concerts at Cardiff's St David's Hall, culminating in a patriotic flag-waving Last Night of the Welsh Proms.

Gŵyl Machynlleth (August): Held alongside Machynlleth's popular fringe festival, the auditorium of The Tabernacle, a renovated Wesleyan chapel which retains its pews for seats, hosts a series of events including choral singing and chamber music.

BBC Proms in the Park (September): In 2005, Wales joined with Hyde Park in hosting its own Last Night of the Proms in the Park in Swansea, the grand finale of the eight-week UK-wide summer celebration of orchestral music. While it has no permanent home and can relocate annually, Swansea's Singleton Park has remained the most popular choice of venue. Music is supplied by the BBC National Orchestra of Wales and BBC National Chorus of Wales, who are joined by guest soloists.

Swansea International Festival (October): Founded in 1948 as the Swansea Festival of Music and the Arts and rebranded in 2015, the two-week festival brings classical music, opera, drama, dance and art to venues across Swansea. The biggest concerts take place at the Brangwyn Hall, and the festival's summer launch is also the setting for the annual John Fussell Award for Young Musicians, which is – financially – one of Wales's largest music awards.

UNIQUELY WELSH EVENTS

The Six Nations Championship (February/March): Rugby is, symbolically at least, the national sport of Wales, and the experience of watching it with a capacity crowd of over 70,000 singing the national anthem is enough to give anyone goosebumps. The national stadium is situated bang in the middle of Cardiff, and when the boys in red run out for a competitive match in their annual showdown against England, France, Ireland, Italy or Scotland, match days take on a carnival-like atmosphere.

Wonderwool Wales (April): Wales' wool and natural fibre festival at the Royal Welsh Showground is an annual party for all things woolly, offering artisan goods from the producers themselves and an opportunity to get hands-on and learn a few tips in the workshops.

Machynlleth Comedy Festival (April/May): Comedy is booming in Wales, with clubs and festivals popping up across the country, and Welsh-language comedy an increasingly important part of the

National Eisteddfod. The annual highlight is the Machynlleth Comedy Festival, launched in 2010 and set in a series of intimate venues across the town, which has become a firm fixture in the diaries of many leading touring acts.

Pride Cymru (August): Launched in 1999 as Cardiff Mardi Gras, Wales' largest LGBT pride parade and festival is a vibrant party that sees people from around the world take to the streets of Cardiff for a celebration of equality and diversity, before gathering at the festival ground for the main event.

ONLY IN LLANWRTYD WELLS ...

The small town of Llanwrtyd Wells in Powys has firmly established itself as the place to go for some of the quirkiest events to be found outdoors in Wales – or anywhere else in the world for that matter.

The World Bog Snorkelling Championships is a major draw, in which competitors, some in fancy dress, attempt to swim though a muddy 133m peat bog in the shortest time.

The Man versus Horse Marathon is, as the name suggests, a peculiar 22-mile countryside marathon in which racers try to outrun those on horseback. Held every June, the event began – as these things do – as a conversation in a pub in 1980, and with the horse riders at a clear advantage, a rolling prize fund was established for the eventual victor. When cycling was permitted, the first human winner triumphed on two wheels in 1989, while the first runner to beat his equestrian competitor on foot claimed the £25,000 jackpot in 2004.

The World Alternative Games were established in 2012 in response to London's Summer Olympics, and incorporated the already-established annual events with ingenious new challenges like Worm Charming and the Wife Carrying Championships. The now biennial competition attracts competitors from across the world, and also includes games designed for children such as Pooh Sticks and rock-paper-scissors.

FOOD AND DRINK

Practical and regional, traditional Welsh food was derived from the land, and was required to survive long periods in storage and to sustain the workforce.

Cawl – or lobscouse in parts of North Wales – is seen as the country's national dish, a hardy vegetable and meat-based stew which dates back to the fourteenth century.

A vegetarian alternative is **cawl cennin** (leek cawl), while other popular meat-free dishes include the cheese and leek-based **Glamorgan sausages** and the ever-popular **Welsh rarebit**, made from a melted cheese sauce poured over toasted bread.

For those on the shore, seafood delicacies include the famous **Penclawdd cockles, Conwy's mussels,** and the once-plentiful **Mumbles oysters.** A full Welsh breakfast is not dissimilar to those from the other home nations, but with the noticeable addition of cockles and **laverbread** – boiled and minced seaweed which was described by Richard Burton as 'Welshman's caviar'.

Cakes which can readily be sampled today include **Welsh cakes,** made from flour and flavoured with fruit and spices and best served warm, and the resilient fruit cake **bara brith** (speckled bread).

Welsh cakes.

Regional food festivals can be found across the country, the largest of which is held in **Abergavenny** every September. **Cardiff International Food and Drink Festival** is described as the UK's largest free outdoor festival, with the three-day event boasting Wales's biggest street food piazza. Other food festivals of note include **Llangollen, Mold, Cowbridge, Neath** and **Narberth**.

Caerphilly's **The Big Cheese Festival** opens in July with a grand fireworks display and combines food and drink with historical re-enactment demonstrations, while **The Really Wild Food and Countryside Festival** at the working National Trust farm Pwll Caerog makes the most of its surroundings by offering walks, live music in a barn, and a particularly messy mud run every May.

Seafood highlights include Conwy's **Gwledd Conwy Feast** which takes place during its mussel season in October; the **Cardigan Bay Seafood Festival** in the picturesque seaside resort of Aberaeron, which is also home to The Hive's famous honey ice cream; and the all-encompassing **Pembrokeshire Fish Week**, which includes activities for those who, not content with just shopping and tasting, want to pick up a rod and hook their own catch of the day.

Breweries and microbreweries offer their own regional varieties of ale, the most prominent being Cardiff's **Brains Brewery**, which produces the infamous Brains SA, nicknamed skull attack for its morning-after effects. With its brewery tours and memorable marketing campaigns, it is the nearest Wales has to rivalling Ireland's Guinness brand.

Regular beer festivals organised by **CAMRA** (Campaign for Real Ale) include events in **Newport, Swansea,** and the **Great Welsh Beer and Cider Festival in Cardiff**. The ten-day **Mid Wales Beer Festival** takes place in Llanwrtyd Wells during November, kicking off with the **Real Ale Wobble** in which cyclists of all abilities can join in a fun ride through the countryside, stopping off at check points to sample a beer along the way. The town also hosts the **Saturnalia Real Ale Ramble** in January, in which warming ales can be picked up while walking the old Roman roads.

When it comes to spirits, **Penderyn Distillery** lead the way with their own visitor centre in the Brecon Beacons. Famous for their single malt whisky, their other brands include gin and vodka.

THE ROYAL WELSH SHOW

One of the country's most prominent events is the Royal Welsh Show (Sioe Frenhinol Cymru), a leading UK farming showcase which is said to be the biggest agricultural show in Europe. Royal by name, royal by nature, members of the Royal Family are often seen in attendance, with the Prince of Wales being a regular visitor.

Established in 1904 by the Royal Welsh Agricultural Society, the four-day show, which takes place every July at the Royal Welsh Showground in Llanelwedd, just outside Builth Wells, is the scene of hotly contested livestock competitions, and has expanded to incorporate all areas of rural life, including outdoor activities and live entertainment.

EXPLORING NATIONAL MUSEUM WALES

The Welsh government-sponsored National Museum Wales (Amgueddfa Cymru) has seven unique associated museums across the country, each focusing on a distinct aspect of Welsh history and culture.

National Museum Cardiff: The capital city's museum houses a vast collection of archaeology and geology curiosities, natural history galleries featuring the world's largest leatherback turtle, and is located in the same building as the National Museum of Art, famed for its impressive collection of Impressionist and national works of art.

St Fagans National History Museum, Cardiff: Set in St Fagans Castle, the Museum of Welsh Life is an open-air museum that spans 500 years of Welsh history. Attractions include historical buildings from across the country relocated to its parkland, traditional workers, livestock, and indoor galleries that house a collection of rare cultural curiosities.

Big Pit National Coal Museum, Blaenavon: The National Mining Museum of Wales was a fully functioning coal mine until 1980, and now offers visitors the chance to explore the coalface, and to don a torch-lit helmet and experience going deep underground with former miners.

National Wool Museum, Llandysul: The village of Dre-fach Felindre was a major player in the Welsh wool industry, producing everything from shawls to bedcovers for a global market. The tradition is kept alive today not only by preserving the past, but by continuing to create fabrics in the working mill. It also houses the National Textile Collection.

National Slate Museum, Llanberis: The preserved Victorian workshops at the foot of the Dinorwig Quarry offer a glimpse back to Wales' industrial past, with demonstrations from craftsmen, forges, and an original Hunslet steam train which once transported the slate.

National Roman Legion Museum, Caerleon: A remarkably intact amphitheatre, which was known as King Arthur's Round Table in the Middle Ages, sits at the heart of the National Roman Legion Museum, which includes well-preserved structures, galleries, uniforms, artefacts, and the oldest writing in Wales on a wooden first-century tablet.

National Waterfront Museum, Swansea: Swansea's National Waterfront Museum utilises the latest multimedia technologies to bring the industrial and maritime heritage of the city to life in fifteen themed galleries across two linked buildings – a modern slate and glass construction connected to a listed warehouse that overlooks the marina.

2

WELSH LITERATURE

THE EARLY POETS

Being a bard in the Middle Ages was a serious business.

Y Cynfeirdd, Wales' earliest poets who began composing verse when the Welsh language was in its infancy, were patronised by royalty and society's elite to write praise poetry – essentially a medieval form of marketing that would allow tales of their mighty deeds to be spread far and wide.

An oral tradition until the scribes of later generations recorded their words, the works of only two sixth-century poets are known to survive: **Taliesin** and **Aneirin**.

The fourteenth-century manuscript *Llyfr Taliesin* (*The Book of Taliesin*), which can be found at the National Library of Wales, Aberystwyth, contains fifty-six early Welsh poems, twelve of which have been attributed to Taliesin, which would have been composed for King Urien of Rheged and his son Owain mab Urien.

Taliesin – or his namesake, at least – became the subject of legend himself in *Hanes Taliesin* (*Historia Taliesin*), a sixteenth-century work by or about the court poet. In his fantastical origin story, a young Gwion Bach, a servant of the enchantress Ceridwen, is granted infinite wisdom after swallowing three drops of a potion reserved for his mistress. A chase ensues between an enraged Ceridwen and a fleeing Gwion, and the pair transform into various creatures in a magical game of cat-and-mouse – a hare and a greyhound, a fish and an otter, a bird and a hawk, and finally a grain of corn and a black hen. Ceridwen falls pregnant after eating the corn, and the discarded newborn baby grows up to become Taliesin.

Aneirin, who also composed for King Urien and whose *Llyfr Aneirin* (*The Book of Aneirin*) can also be found at the National Library of

Wales, composed the long poem Y Gododdin, assembled from a series of elegies following the Battle of Catraeth in 598 in which the king's son was killed.

Dated 1265, *Llyfr Aneirin* is also notable for containing the first mention, if assumed to date from the sixth century, of one of the most enduring characters to emerge from Welsh history: King Arthur.

KING ARTHUR: MAN OR MYTH?

Long before the romantic revivals and big-budget Hollywood movies, *The Historia Brittonum*, thought to have been written in 828 by the Welsh monk Nennius, is considered to be the first written reference by date to the character that we now know as King Arthur.

Illustration of King Arthur from Howard Pyle's *The Story of King Arthur and His Knights*, 1903.

While not believed to be an entirely historically accurate manuscript, it details the twelve battles fought and won by Arthur, who is not referred to as a king, but as a war leader, warrior or soldier.

It also contains references to his son Amr and dog Cabal, and the legend of Vortigern, who attempts to build a fortress in Dinas Emrys above a secret pool in which two dragons are fighting – the white Saxon dragon and the red Welsh dragon, who now adorns the Welsh flag.

The tale was further embellished by Geoffrey of Monmouth in his *Historia Regum Britanniae* (History of the Kings of Britain), which popularised the idea of Arthur as the king of Britain who fought off the Saxon invaders. Written around 1136, it introduced many reoccuring characters and places into Arthurian mythology including Merlin, who is based on the Welsh legend Myrddin Wyllt (Merlin the Wild). The wizard is said to have come from Carmarthen, and his name can be found in the second half of the town's Welsh name, Caerfyrddin – the fortress of Merlin.

Dated around 1250, the oldest surviving manuscript written solely in Welsh is the *Black Book of Carmarthen*. Principally a collection of poems, it contains early references to King Arthur, who can also be found in the Welsh Triads, the oldest of which is also thought to date from the thirteenth century.

One theory for the source of Arthur's name suggests that it is a combination of the Welsh words for bear (*arth*) and gold (*aur*). His surname, Pendragon, is the title of chief dragon or dragon's head.

GERALD'S JOURNEY THROUGH WALES

From the snowy peaks of Snowdonia to St Davids' majestic cathedral, for a first-hand account of medieval Wales from a man who travelled the land and recorded all that he saw we can turn to Gerald of Wales (*c*.1146 – *c*.1223), whose 1191 *Itinerarium Cambriae* (Journey Through Wales) and 1194 *Descriptio Cambriae* (Description of Wales) now serve as invaluable historical documents of the period.

The son of a nobleman, the chronicler was born Gerald de Barri (Gerallt Gymroin) at Manorbier Castle, a Norman fortress in Pembrokeshire which is now open to the public.

Having become Archdeacon of Brecon in 1174 – his predecessor was conveniently dismissed after his secret mistress was exposed by Gerald – he was chosen to succeed his uncle as the Bishop of St Davids, but was denied by King Henry II of England who favoured having a more trustworthy ally in such a powerful position.

The king's intervention would instead launch Gerald's literary career when, while working as a royal clerk, he accompanied Henry's son John on a tour of Ireland, where he recorded his travels in his first work, 1187's *Topographia Hibernica* (Topography of Ireland).

The following year, the Archbishop of Canterbury, Baldwin of Forde, set off to Wales on a recruitment drive for the Third Crusade, and Gerald was again offered the opportunity of travel. From the mundane to the miraculous, Gerald records the events of the expedition to his homeland – and more besides – in a far from unbiased account steeped in folklore and mythology.

POETS OF THE NOBILITY

Following the conquest of Wales by Edward I of England and the beheading of Welsh ruler Llywelyn ap Gruffudd, the period known as the Poets of the Princes gave way to the Poets of the Nobility, who were commissioned to compose praise poetry for the aristocracy rather than royalty.

Poetry at the time was regulated by the Guild of Poets, and would-be bards would have to serve a nine-year apprenticeship before being able to ply their trade, which included a mastery of the complex forms of cynghanedd (harmony), an intricate set of rules concerning stress, alliteration and rhyme.

Cynghanedd, in its most simplest form, can be divided into twenty-four measures, known as Y Pedwar Mesur ar Hugain, with five types of englyn (short stanzas), fifteen types of awdl (a long poem with a single end-rhyme), and four types of cywydd, the favoured form of the Cywyddwyr which included writing uneven-syllable lines in rhyming couplets.

Foremost among the Cywyddwyr was **Dafydd ap Gwilym** (*c*.1315/20 – *c*.1350/1370), Wales', if not Europe's, greatest Middle Age poet, who broke new ground by composing poetry on a novel subject – himself.

By looking inside, he explored his feelings of love and affection, and injected humour into his writing, which was not always pure and clean, with lustful thoughts for the pious women in church, and an ill-fated late night rendezvous in a tavern. Thought to have been born to noble parents in Brogynin, Penrhyn-coch, Ceredigion, a memorial to the poet can be found in the grounds of Strata Florida Abbey.

Other notable poets using the form during the period include **Iolo Goch**, a cywydd forerunner who composed for Owain Glyndŵr, and **Siôn Cent**, who also broke with tradition to focus on writing about his Christian faith. **Gwerful Mechain** also wrote works of a religious nature, along with the unlikely combination of erotic poetry, penning the infamous Cywydd y Cedor – Ode to the Pubic Hair.

Wagstaff's statue of Dafydd ap Gwilym at Cardiff City Hall.

THE MABINOGION

Illustration of Branwen with the drudwy (starling) from
Charlotte Guest's translation of the *Mabinogion*, 1877.

Interweaving myth, folklore and history into eleven weird and
wonderful tales, the *Mabinogion* is arguably the most important piece
of prose literature written in the Welsh language, made all the more
remarkable considering that it originates from oral stories believed to
date from the eleventh century.

While their exact date remains the subject of scholarly debate,
in written form they are derived from the fourteenth-century
manuscripts *Llyfr Coch Hergest* (The Red Book of Hergest) and *Llyfr
Gwyn Rhydderch* (The White Book of Rhydderch), with modern
English-language translations beginning at the turn of the nineteenth
century when William Owen Pughe published a handful of the stories.

It was Lady Charlotte Elizabeth Guest of Lincolnshire, the wife of
Welsh industrialist John Josiah Guest, who reignited a passion for the
stories when, inspired by the Gothic fiction and chivalrous romantic
tales of the period, she undertook an ambitious bilingual translation
of the works while living in Merthyr Tydfil.

Published between 1838 and 1845, she was the first to assemble the
eleven stories which comprise the *Mabinogion* into a single volume,
which can be divided into three sections: The Four Branches of the
Mabinogi (Pedair Cainc y Mabinogi), native tales and Arthurian tales.

The Four Branches of the Mabinogi, from which the collection
derives its name after Guest picked up a scribal error which had
incorrectly written mabinogi as mabinogion, are seen as a single work
with a common theme running throughout.

Wildly imaginative but usually with a moral to the tale, in Pwyll, Prince of Dyfed, the prince visits the kingdom of Annwn following an ill-fated hunting expedition, and later marries Rhiannon, who is accused of cannibalism when their son mysteriously disappears. In Branwen, daughter of Llŷr, the title character is locked into an abusive marriage to the King of Ireland, which results in the two countries going to war. In Manawydan, son of Llŷr, the repercussions of the war are dealt with, and a curse is lifted from Dyfed by a bishop when Manawydan agrees to spare the life of a mouse – which turns out to be the bishop's wife. While in Math, son of Mathonwy, the King of Gwynedd is able to detect a girl's virginity with a wave of his wand – a handy skill, as he will die if he doesn't permanently rest his feet in a virgin's lap when he isn't fighting.

The four native tales included by Guest are The Dream of Macsen Wledig, Lludd and Llyfelys, and two that directly relate to Arthurian legend, Culhwch and Olwen, the first story to feature Arthur as its hero, and The Dream of Rhonabwy.

The three Arthurian romances, The Lady of the Fountain, Peredur, son of Efrog and Gereint, son of Erbin, can all draw parallels with the earlier works of French poet Chrétien de Troyes.

Guest's translation remained the definite version until Gwyn Jones and Thomas Jones' popular 1948 translation became standard, with Jeffrey Gantz's translation following in 1976 and Patrick Ford translating The Four Branches of the Mabinogi and the native tales a year later.

The stories of the *Mabinogion* continue to inspire today, with Seren launching the *New Stories from the Mabinogion* series in 2009 in which the tales are reimagined by contemporary writers, and are often adapted for the stage and screen, possibly most notably to a global audience in Disney's *The Black Cauldron* (1985), an animated adventure based on Lloyd Alexander's *Mabinogion*-inspired *The Chronicles of Prydain*.

THE WELSH BIBLE

A new age of print was heralded when Sir John Price of Brecon's *Yn y llyvyr hwnn* ... (In this book ...), dated 1546, became the first book to be published in Welsh. And when the most important work to be printed in the language followed in the autumn of 1588, it was received like a gift from heaven.

Not only did the Welsh Bible confer equal status onto the language, it is credited by many for its very survival by allowing the pious people of Wales to finally read – and scrutinise – the scriptures for themselves.

The New Testament had been translated in 1567 by William Salesbury, but it was **William Morgan** (1545–1604) who set about translating the Old Testament as well, which he combined with a revised edition of Salesbury's earlier release to form the complete Bible.

Born and raised in Tŷ Mawr Wybrnant house near Betws-y-Coed, which is now cared for by the National Trust, Morgan studied at Cambridge before taking up posts in parishes across Wales, starting in Llanbadarn Fawr before moving to Welshpool and Llanrhaeadr-ym-Mochnant, where he married and set about his life's greatest work.

Having spent a year in London to supervise its printing, Morgan became a hero overnight when the Bible arrived in Wales. Appointed the Bishop of Llandaff soon after, he again revised the words of Salesbury in the *Book of Common Prayer* (1599), before moving to St Asaph where he spent the rest of his life.

Morgan was in the process of revising his own Bible at the time of his death, which was completed by Bishop Richard Parry and Dr John Davies and published in 1620.

The title page from the first Welsh Bible, 1588.

NATIONALISM AND
THE FUTURE OF WRITING IN WELSH

By the turn of the twentieth century, English writing had established a strong foothold in Wales, but aided by the emergence of the University of Wales colleges and the formation of a National Library of Wales in Aberystwyth, there was a flourishing of Welsh writers keen to restore their heritage and air their strong political and spiritual views.

In the second half of the nineteenth century, **Daniel Owen** (1836–1895) from Mold emerged as the first leading Welsh-language novelist, notably for his second novel *Rhys Lewis* (1885) and its sequel *Enoc Huws* (1891), both social commentaries on the characters, religion and hypocrisy that he saw in his hometown.

Seeking to 'restore the Old Country to its former glory', **O.M. Edwards** (1858–1920) from Llanuwchllyn, Gwynedd, was determined to resist what he saw as the Anglicisation of Welsh culture. Having worn the Welsh Not himself at school, upon becoming the Chief Inspector of Schools for Wales he fought hard for a Welsh-language education system, and wrote books for children along with works on travel, history and literature.

He was far from alone in his endeavour, with the scholar **John Morris-Jones** publishing several important works on Wales' literary heritage, including examinations of the rules of cynghanedd, the works of Taliesin, and *A Welsh Grammar* (1913), while the academic and translator **T. Gwynn Jones** heralded a new age of cynghanedd with his heroic National Eisteddfod-winning poem Ymadawiad Arthur (The Departure of Arthur) in 1902.

Among the patriotic ministers who raised their voices from the pulpits were **Emrys ap Iwan,** who considered himself a Welsh European, the popular hymn writer and archdruid **Howell 'Elfed' Lewis,** and **Robert 'Silyn' Roberts** who, along with **W.J. Gruffydd,** published the influential collection of poetry *Telynegion* in 1900.

The Christian faith was central to many writing verse at the time. The scholar and critic **D. Gwenallt Jones**, who took his bardic name after the village of Alltwen, battled with his own complex ideas of piety and nationalism in five increasingly intense books of poetry, epitomised in the posthumous *Y Coed* (The Trees, 1969). A double National Eisteddfod chair winner for his awdls Y Mynach (The Monk, 1926) and Breuddwyd y Bardd (The Poet's Dream, 1931), a third poem, Y Sant (The Saint), was considered to be a potential winner in 1928, but was deemed 'morally depraved' by the judges.

Others who excelled at the National Eisteddfod include **Gwilym R. Jones**, a steadfast supporter of the Presbyterian Church of Wales, and the only person to have won all three literary awards – the crown in 1936, the chair in 1938, and the prose medal for his novel *Y Purdan* (Purgatory) in 1941. **T.H. Parry-Williams**, who was the first poet to win the crown and chair double, explored the ambiguity of the notion of hiraeth, a unique Welsh word for nostalgia and longing, in his first collection *Cerddi* (Poems, 1931) and his most famous poem Hon (This).

But despite only publishing a single book of his own verse in his lifetime, the foremost poet to emerge from this period was **Waldo Williams** (1904–1971), a deeply religious man and a staunch pacifist who was imprisoned for his beliefs during the Korean War for refusing to pay income tax.

Williams' poems, which adhered to the rules of cynghanedd, were written about the people and for the people, and often reflected his ideal of a united society and themes of Welsh nationalism. One particularly powerful collection was written in response to the government's decision to set up a firing range in the farming community of his beloved Preseli Hills, Pembrokeshire, where a stone monument to Williams now stands in Rhosfach, Mynachlog-ddu.

TÂN YN LLŶN

A significant turning point for nationalism, and for Welsh literature, came in 1936 when The Penyberth Three – Plaid Cymru members **Saunders Lewis, D.J. Williams** and **Lewis Valentine** – were prosecuted for setting fire to parts of an RAF bombing school in protest of it being built on the scenic Llŷn Peninsular, a traditional, Christian, Welsh-speaking area.

The protest became known as Tân yn Llŷn (Fire in Llŷn), and having reported themselves to the police afterwards the trio were sentenced to nine months imprisonment, only to be greeted as national heroes by a crowd of around 12,000 on their return from Wormwood Scrubs.

Saunders would go on to establish himself as one of the country's leading, if controversial, literary and political figures, while Williams continued to write stories firmly rooted in the community values of his birthplace, the village of Rhydcymerau in Carmarthenshire. Valentine remained active as a political voice and pastor, and wrote the hymn Gweddi dros Gymru (A Prayer for Wales) to Sibelius' *Finlandia Hymn*, which has been described as the second Welsh national anthem.

D.J. Williams, Lewis Valentine and Saunders Lewis on the Llosgi'r Ysgol Fomio / The Burning of the Bombing School stone. (Alan Fryer)

The incident also spurred other writers into action, such as **R. Williams Parry**, who had established himself as Y Bardd y Haf (The Bard of Summer) with his 1910 National Eisteddfod-winning poem Yr Haf (The Summer), but returned to writing with a newfound fury following the events.

Novelist **Emyr Humphreys** from Prestatyn, who would write over twenty novels including the Hawthornden Prize-winning *A Toy Epic* (1958), launched his literary career with a book directly inspired by the events, *Little Kingdom* (1946).

THE SCARS OF WAR

One of the most iconic pieces of writing to be inspired by the First World War is **David Jones'** Hawthornden Prize-winning part-poem, part-prose modernist epic *In Parenthesis* (1937), which symbolically draws inspiration from a wide range of literary sources, including the ancient Welsh texts *Y Gododdin* and the *Mabinogion*. Born to a Welsh-speaking father in Kent, Jones was also an accomplished painter, and served on the Western Front with the Royal Welch Fusiliers.

Despite being a pacifist, Ellis Humphrey Evans, a shepherd from Trawsfynydd better known by his bardic name **Hedd Wyn** (Blessed Peace), enlisted for the army during the First World War to spare his younger brother the same fate. Yet the fledgling poet paid the ultimate price in 1917 during the Battle of Passchendaele, and was posthumously awarded the National Eisteddfod's chair cloaked in a black sheet for his poem Yr Arwr (The Hero).

Alun Lewis from Cwmaman was another Welsh pacifist whose life was cut tragically short during the Second World War. Soon after the publication of his first poetry and short story collections, he was found dead from a gunshot wound to the head while serving in Burma in 1944. Despite being classed as an accident, it is widely known to have been suicide – the revolver was still in his hand.

THE CADWGAN CIRCLE

During the Second World War, a group of Welsh-language writers and thinkers in the Rhondda Valleys banded together to form the Cylch Cadwgan – the Cadwgan Circle.

The literary and political avant-garde movement was founded by the poet and Egyptologist **J. Gwyn Griffiths** from Porth and his German wife **Käte Bosse-Griffiths**, a fellow Egyptologist who he had met while studying in Oxford.

Their home served as the group's meeting place, and fellow members included the experimental poet **Euros Bowen**, innovative playwright **James Kitchener Davies**, modernist writer **Pennar Davies** and the prodigious writer of industrial Rhondda **Rhydwen Williams**.

THE SLATE MINES OF NORTH WALES

It was the slate quarry mines of North Wales that inspired three of the leading Welsh-language industrial writers.

Kate Roberts, the Brenhines ein Llên (the Queen of our Literature), captured the hardships of life for a slate quarry family in her 1936 novel *Traed mewn Cyffion* (Feet in Chains), which is seen as the start of the industrial tradition of writing in Wales. Born in Cae'r Gors in the Caernarfon village of Rhosgadfan, which has now been restored as a heritage centre, the firm nationalist met her future husband Morris T. Williams at a Plaid Cymru meeting, and settled in Denbigh where they bought the Welsh-language printers and publishers Gwasg Gee.

Thomas Rowland Hughes, whose father worked as a quarryman in his native Llanberis, also had first-hand experience of life around the slate industry. His novel *William Jones* (1944), in which a quarryman seeks a new life in the valleys of South Wales, contains the line 'Cadw dy blydi chips!' ('Keep your bloody chips!'), which has the distinction of being the first time a swear word was used in modern-day Welsh writing.

For **Caradog Prichard**, who had established himself as a poet by winning the National Eisteddfod three years in a row between 1927 and 1929, the slate mines around his hometown of Bethesda provided the backdrop to what is now considered to be one of the classics of Welsh literature, 1961's *Un Nos Ola Leuad* (One Moonlit Night). Numerous translations of the almost indescribable story of an unnamed boy's development into adulthood, characterised by insanity, violence and sexual transgressions, have popularised the book across the world.

EARLY WELSH WRITING IN ENGLISH

The first known English language work to be written by a Welsh person is **Ieuan ap Hywel Swrdwal's** poem The Hymn to the Virgin, written in the awdl form in 1470, but a strong case exists for the honour to be given to **Sir John Clanvowe's** *The Book of Cupid, God of Love or The Cuckoo and the Nightingale*, which was written in the fourteenth century and had previously been attributed to his friend and inspiration Geoffrey Chaucer.

In the eighteenth century the poet **John Dyer** from Llanfynnydd, Carmarthenshire, proved to be something of a one-hit wonder with his poem Grongar Hill, yet was immortalised in a sonnet by key English romantic poet **William Wordsworth** in To The Poet, John Dyer. Wordsworth was no stranger to Wales, and it was during a return visit to the Welsh Borders in 1798 that he felt compelled to compose one of his more well-known poems, Tintern Abbey, which he claimed was formed entirely in his head during the walk before he even had time to sit down and put pen to paper.

In 1799, **Ann of Swansea** – Ann Hatton from Worcester – settled in her adopted hometown from which she would derive her writing alias. Her often Gothic stories and poems drew heavily, if not always favourably, from her Welsh surroundings.

T.J. Llewelyn Prichard, a writer and actor whose colourful life is shrouded in mystery, re-established one of the country's more enduring folk heroes in *The Adventures and Vagaries of Twm Shôn Catti* (1882), said to be the first Welsh novel written in English. Believed to have been born in the village of Trallong around 1790 and to have died in Swansea in 1862 after drunkenly falling into his own fireplace, he was forced to give up acting and concentrate on writing after a sword fight or fencing accident resulted in the end of his nose being chopped off, which he concealed with a wax replica attached to his glasses.

National Eisteddfod-winning romantic novelist **Allen Raine**, the pen name of Anne Adalisa Beynon Puddicombe from Newcastle Emlyn, was rejected by several publishers in London before her first English-language novel *A Welsh Singer* (1896) finally saw the light of day. Her books would go on to sell millions of copies.

At the same period, Wales' leading horror and fantasy writer – as well as mystic, journalist and translator – **Arthur Machen** was also causing a stir in the English capital, due to his associations with the decadent movement which had been rocked by the scandal surrounding Oscar Wilde. Machen's work was deeply influenced by his upbringing in Caerleon, where the Roman amphitheatre and mystical countryside fired an imagination that would conjure up tales of ghosts, nymphs and fairies, and the most menacing evil of all – *The Great God Pan* (1894).

The novella has been described by Stephen King, the world's most successful horror writer, as 'Maybe the best in the English language', and along with *The White People* (1894) was also an influence on director Guillermo del Toro's Academy Award-winning film *Pan's Labyrinth* (2006). Machen also gave birth to the legend of the Angels of Mons in his short story *The Bowmen* (1914), who are said to have protected the British soldiers during the First World War.

A FLOURISHING OF WELSH WRITING IN ENGLISH

Welsh writing in English flourished at the start of the twentieth century, and foremost among the writers of the period was the provocative **Caradoc Evans** from Rhydlewis, Cardiganshire, who, while garnering praise from the English press, was less well thought of at home, dubbed 'the most hated man in Wales' by the *Western Mail*.

In 1915, his first collection of short stories *My People* lifted the veil on the romanticised image of Wales that the country was keen to project to the outside world, portraying it as a land plagued by malice, religious hypocrisy and poverty. His second release, 1916's *Capel Sion*, was withdrawn from circulation in Welsh bookshops, while in 1923 the police were called to keep the peace following the hostile reaction of Welsh theatregoers at the opening of his play *Taffy* in London.

Writer and poet **W.H. Davies** from Pillgwenlly, Newport, spent years travelling America as a tramp, and the pivotal moment for his literary career came in 1899 when, while trying to jump onto a train bound for Ontario, he slipped and his foot was crushed underneath the train, resulting in his right leg being amputated below the knee. With his old way of living gone, Davies turned his attention to writing, and was soon catching the eye of the publishers, and London society, with his self-published poetry and his recollection of those years drifting in *The Autobiography of a Super-Tramp* (1908).

For the writers on the border with England, the duality of the cultures fuelled their fiction, as exemplified in *Country Dance* (1932) by **Margiad Evans**, who was born on the English side but switched after marrying a Welshman. Journalist **Geraint Goodwin** from Llanllwchaiarn, who was motivated to write his first novel *Call Back Yesterday* (1935) after being diagnosed with tuberculosis, also turned to the border for his darkly humorous romantic fictional debut *The Heyday in the Blood* (1936).

Cardiff-born journalist **Howard Spring** found success on the silver screen when Hollywood filmed *My Son, My Son!* (1937) starring Madeleine Carroll, and his most well-known work, 1940's *Fame is the Spur* with Sir Michael Redgrave taking the lead.

THE FIRST ROCK STAR POET

If the shadow of one writer looms larger over the literature of Wales than any other, it would be the cherub-faced shadow of Swansea's Rimbaud of Cwmdonkin Drive, the first 'rock star poet' and the second most quoted British poet after Shakespeare, **Dylan Marlais Thomas** (27 October 1914 – 9 November 1953).

While his words should, and do, speak for themselves, his legendary personal life could still supply enough anecdotes to fill a book ten times the size of this one – and most of them would be true.

There was the public fist fight with Augustus John over the painter's mistress and the poet's future wife Caitlin Macnamara, to whom he proposed on their first meeting with his head drunkenly resting in her lap. Or his near-death experience following an altercation with a machine gun-wielding army captain in New Quay, who shot up the Thomas' wooden house with the family inside. Or even the time during an American tour that he crashed his car into Charlie Chaplin's tennis court, before unceremoniously relieving himself in the silent actor's pot plant.

And it was while on an ill-fated tour of America in 1953 that he was said to have claimed that 'I've had eighteen straight whiskies, I think that's the record' at New York's Hotel Chelsea. Two days later, he was rushed by ambulance to St Vincent's Hospital with breathing difficulties, in a comatose state from which he would never awake.

Dylan Thomas. (Nora Summers / Dylan's Bookstore Collection)

Practically all of Thomas' back catalogue can be considered essential reading. His works of prose, from the nostalgia of *A Child's Christmas in Wales* (a radio broadcast from 1952) to the autobiographical *Portrait of the Artist as a Young Dog* (1940), serve as a gentle introduction to the bard's writing, while his poetry, now easily available as complete collections, include the oft-quoted masterpieces And death shall have no dominion (1933) and Do not go gentle into that good night (1952).

For many, Thomas' definitive work is his play for voices, *Under Milk Wood*, first broadcast in 1954. Set in the fictional fishing village of Llareggub – yes, bugger all backwards – a narrator lays bare the innermost feelings and desires of a colourful cast of Welsh caricatures, from the blind Captain Cat who is haunted by his drowned shipmates, to single mother Polly Garter who yearns for her lost love.

Anyone thinking of setting out on a Dylan Thomas pilgrimage will have no shortage of places to visit in Wales, which is made all the more appealing by the fact that Thomas lived and wrote in some of the country's more picturesque locations, like the stunning Dylan Thomas Trail in New Quay which formed the basis of much of *Under Milk Wood*.

His birthplace at 5 Cwmdonkin Drive, Swansea, is open to the public, and overlooks Cwmdonkin Park, a constant source of inspiration for the young poet. The Dylan Thomas Centre in the city centre houses an excellent permanent exhibition, while Swansea Little Theatre regularly stages plays at the Dylan Thomas Theatre, outside of which can be found a statue of the poet himself, with an accompanying statue of Captain Cat on the opposite side of the marina.

Possibly the most iconic location associated with Thomas is his writing shed, a replica of which now tours the country, and which can be found alongside the Dylan Thomas Boathouse in Laugharne. The small town in Carmarthenshire is also Thomas' final resting place, which is marked by a plain white cross bearing his name, on the reverse of which is the name of his wife who lays beside him in the graveyard of St Martin's church.

THE KARDOMAH GANG

The so-called Kardomah Gang was the collective name given to Dylan Thomas and his bohemian contemporaries who gathered for coffee and cigarettes in the Swansea café during the 1930s where, according to Thomas' *Return Journey*, they discussed 'Einstein and Epstein, Stravinsky and Greta Garbo, death and religion, Picasso and girls'.

Its members included the journalist and poet **Charles Fisher**, writer **John Prichard**, composer **Daniel Jones**, artists **Alfred Janes** and **Mervyn Levy**, teacher **Mabley Owen**, musician **Tom Warner**, and the poet **Vernon Watkins**.

After Thomas, Watkins emerged as the most prominent man of words from the gang, although he lived a far more conservative life than his friend. Born in Maesteg, he settled in Pennard, Gower, where the peninsula served as his muse as he juggled writing with working as a manager at Lloyds Bank. Watkins' poetry is heavy with symbolism, and it is thought that a nervous breakdown led to a perpetual search for some kind of meaning to life through words.

Maintaining a close friendship throughout their lives, Watkins was godfather to Thomas' eldest son Llewelyn, and Thomas was to be Watkins' best man at his wedding to Gwen – but he failed to turn up at the church. There is a story of the time that Watkins asked Thomas to post his poetry to the publisher, but before dispatching it Thomas 'improved' it with a few tweaks of his own. Upon discovering the changes, Watkins visited every bookshop in Swansea with pen in hand to correct the alterations.

The original Kardomah café was based on Castle Street opposite the old *South Wales Evening Post* offices where Thomas and Fisher worked as journalists, but was destroyed during the Second World War. A new Kardomah now stands on Portland Street.

HOW GREEN WAS MY VALLEY

As traditional industry declined in Wales, the deep scars left on the land and communities informed the words of many of the writers who had first-hand experience of the hardships faced by those who saw their way of life evaporating before their eyes.

Jack Jones drew inspiration from the working classes of his native Merthyr Tydfil, with his acclaimed *Rhondda Roundabout* (1934) chronicling valley life during the Great Depression. The theme was also explored by poet **Idris Davies,** who had lost a finger while working as an underground miner, in *Gwalia Deserta* (1938), which includes the verses which formed the lyrics for the folk song 'The Bells of Rhymney' made famous by The Byrds.

Lewis Jones, a political activist who led hunger marches to London and found himself imprisoned during the 1926 General Strike, chronicled the politicisation of a fresh-faced miner in *Cwmardy* (1937) and *We Live* (1939), while **Gwyn Thomas,** the 'true voice of the English-speaking valleys', was motivated by the turbulent times of the Merthyr and Newport uprisings for his novel *All Things Betray Thee* (1949).

The most well-known novel to emerge from this period was **Richard Llewellyn's** *How Green Was My Valley* (1939), in which a strike threatens to tear apart a proud South Wales coal mining family. Llewellyn, who was born to Welsh parents in Middlesex – despite claiming to be from St Davids during his lifetime – found particular success in America, where his book won the favourite novel award at the National Book Awards in 1940, and was adapted for the big screen in the multiple Academy Award-winning film of the same name.

Writing in a similar, if grittier and more grounded vein, was **Alexander Cordell.** Born to an English family in Sri Lanka, he fell in love with Wales after settling in Abergavenny, and perfectly captured the upheaval of the time in his historical Mortymer Saga – *Rape of the Fair Country* (1959), *The Hosts of Rebecca* (1960) and *Song of the Earth* (1969).

One of Wales's most prolific writers, **Rhys Davies**, from Clydach Vale, wrote of the industrial working classes in the lead up to the Great Depression in his trilogy *Honey and Bread* (1935), *A Time to Laugh* (1937) and *Jubilee Blues* (1938). During a five-decade career in which he won the Edgar Allan Poe Award in New York for his collection *The Chosen One* (1967), he produced more than a hundred short stories, twenty novels, three novellas, two topographical books, two plays and an autobiography.

THE SECOND HALF OF THE TWENTIETH CENTURY

A great thinker as well as a great novelist, the Welsh nationalist and a fervent socialist **Raymond Williams** questioned the very concepts of culture and literature in such acclaimed studies as *Culture and Society* (1958) and *Keywords: A Vocabulary of Culture and Society* (1976).

The son of a railway signalman from the close-knit village of Llanvihangel Crucorney in Monmouthshire, his upbringing would form the basis of the first of his six novels, the autobiographical *Border Country* (1960), and establish principles and left-wing ideals that would fuel his life-long preoccupation with a 'long revolution' to put an end to inequality.

Raymond Williams.

It was a Welsh-speaking, Nonconformist childhood in Merthyr Tydfil that informed the works of **Glyn Jones**, who – after some words of encouragement from Dylan Thomas – wrote a collection of short stories *The Blue Bed* (1937). His autobiographical work *The Dragon has Two Tongues* (1968), which examines his friendship with fellow Welsh writers during the world wars, is considered his most significant piece of writing.

Sport, rather than literature, occupied a young **Ron Berry** while growing up in the village of Blaencwm, Rhondda Cynon Taf, and would form the basis of his most popular work, *So Long, Hector Bebb* (1970). Having played football for Swansea Town AFC and dabbled in amateur boxing, a knee injury called time on his sporting activities in 1943. A similar fate was in store for Pembrokeshire-born champion jockey **Dick Francis**, who retired after falling just short of winning the Grand National while riding the Queen Mother's Devon Lock, and became a best-selling crime novelist.

For **Alun Richards**, who had spent time at sea as a Royal Navy seaman, it was the Mumbles lifeboat which inspired his most well-known novel, *Ennal's Point* (1977), which was adapted by the BBC in 1982. Born in Pontypridd, Richards wrote of post-war Wales in his novel *Home to an Empty House* (1973) and his collections of short stories *Dai Country* (1973) and *The Former Miss Merthyr Tydfil* (1976). He also wrote for radio and television, including scripts for the seafaring favourite *The Onedin Line*.

Iris Davies from Swansea, who took her pen name **Iris Gower** from the adjoining peninsula, was a prolific writer of historical romances which were predominantly set in her hometown. She began publishing in the 1970s with *Tudor Tapestry* (1974), but it was 1983's *Copper Kingdom* that proved to be her breakthrough novel.

THE GRITTY REALITY OF THE TWENTY-FIRST CENTURY

In 1998, Pembrokeshire's **Sarah Waters** announced her arrival on the literary scene with the award-winning *Tipping the Velvet*, which explored lesbian themes in Victorian England and has since been adapted for stage, screen, and translated into more than twenty-four languages. Later novels which have also been adapted for television include *Fingersmith* (2002) and *The Night Watch* (2006).

Cardiff author **John Williams** turned to the dark underbelly of his hometown for inspiration for *Five Pubs, Two Bars and a Nightclub* (1999), the first in The Cardiff Trilogy of hardboiled novels and short stories set in the city. His non-fiction includes *Bloody Valentine: A Killing in Cardiff* (1994), the true story of a Cardiff prostitute who was murdered on Valentine's Day.

Dubbed 'the Welsh Irvine Welsh' for his debut novel *Grits* (2000), the darkly satirical, angst-ridden storytelling of Liverpool-born author **Niall Griffiths** was a shot in the arm for Welsh literature at the turn of the twenty-first century. Set in Aberystwyth where Griffiths had studied at university, the semi-autobiographical tale of drugs, crime and promiscuity was followed by the savage coming of age tale *Sheepshagger* (2001).

Fellow English-born writer **Malcolm Pryce** would also put the seaside town on the literary map with his light-hearted Aberystwyth Noir series of novels, which began in 2001 with *Aberystwyth Mon Amour* and chronicles the adventures of Louie Knight, the best – and only – private detective in town.

In 2011, **Owen Sheers** became the first writer-in-residence for a national rugby team, and *Calan*, his non-fiction writing for the Welsh Rugby Union, was published in 2013. Born in Fiji and raised in Abergavenny, Sheers won the Somerset Maugham Award for his 2005 collection of poem's *Skirrid Hill*, and the Wales Book of the Year Award in the same year for his first work of prose, *The Dust Diaries*, an award he would claim again in 2014 for the verse drama *Pink Mist*.

Former BBC Wales Arts and Media correspondent **Jon Gower**, from Llanelli, who has published works of fiction and non-fiction in Welsh and English, also found success at the Wales Book of the Year Award winning the 2012 Welsh Language Wales Book of the Year Prize for his novel *Y Storïwr* (2011).

WALES AND THE MAN BOOKER PRIZE

In 1970, Cardiff-born writer and filmmaker **Bernice Rubens** (1923–2004) became the first woman – and the first Welsh novelist – to win the Man Booker Prize for Fiction. Born to an orthodox Jewish family in Wales, where her Lithuanian father had met her mother whose family had emigrated from Poland, her upbringing would inspire much of her work, including the award-winning *The Elected Member*, in which an amphetamine-addicted member of a tightly-knit Jewish family is confined to a mental institution. Her connection with the Booker Prize continued in 1975 when *A Five Year Sentence* was named as a runner-up, and in 1986 as a judge.

The prolific travel writer, historian and author **Jan Morris**' *Last Letters from Hav* was shortlisted for the award in 1985. Born James Morris in Somerset in 1926 before transitioning to live as a female, the Golden PEN Award recipient is a proud nationalist who identifies with her Welsh heritage, claiming that she only accepted her CBE in 1999 out of politeness.

In 1986, English novelist **Sir Kingsley Amis**, who lectured at the University of Wales in Swansea between 1949 and 1961 and where his son Martin was born, claimed the award for *The Old Devils*. A humorous, if bittersweet satire set in Wales in which a group of retired men spend their time drinking and reminiscing, its central character is the 'professional Welshman' Alun Weaver, who has established a career as an expert on all-things Brydan, a far-from-subtle substitute for Dylan Thomas, who Amis had met and was far from impressed with – as a writer, or as a person.

Cardiff-born **Trezza Azzopardi** was shortlisted for the award in 2000 for her debut novel *The Hiding Place*, which was set in the Maltese community of her native Tiger Bay, while **Nikita Lalwani**, who was born in India and raised in Cardiff, also based her longlisted debut novel *Gifted* (2007), the story of a maths prodigy and their Hindu family, in the Welsh capital.

MODERN-DAY BARDS

In the twentieth century, exceptional English-language translations of traditional Welsh verse, such as **Gwyn Williams**' *Introduction to Welsh Poetry* (1953) and **Tony Conran**'s *Penguin Book of Welsh Verse* (1967), brought the words of Taliesin, Aneirin and Dafydd ap Gwilym to a much wider audience.

Cardiff-born poet, novelist and playwright **Daniel 'Dannie' Abse** (1923–2014) combined writing with a thirty-year career as a chest consultant in London. Born to a Jewish family, themes of identity, religion and politics permeate his work, no more evident than in the semi-autobiographical novel *Ash on a Young Man's Sleeve* (1954). His first volume of poetry *After Every Green Thing* was published in 1949, and he continued to write regularly throughout his life. The loss of his wife Joan in a tragic car accident fuelled the memoir *The Presence* (2007) and the poetry collection *Two for Joy: Scenes from Married Life* (2010).

Fervent nationalism characterised the works of Swansea-born poet **Harri Webb** (1920–1994), such as his humorous four-line poem Ode to the Severn Bridge, written in 1966 to mark the opening of the bridge which connected Wales with England, in which he noted that '… all the tolls collected/ On the English side'. Webb's four volumes of poetry are available as *Collected Poems*.

Nigel Jenkins (1949–2014) from Gorseinon, a constant source of inspiration for young writers with his lecturing and coaching, was a poet who believed he could make a difference with his words. Courting controversy when needed, he spent a week in jail for refusing to pay a fine following a protest outside an American airbase in Pembrokeshire, and after watching the Secretary of State for Wales John Redwood hilariously fumble his way through the Welsh national anthem, he suggested a phonetic version for English speakers which included the chorus: 'Dad! Dad! Why don't you oil Auntie Glad?'

Other poets of note include Neath-born environmentalist **Robert Minhinnick,** who edited *Poetry Wales* for over a decade and twice won the Forward Prize for Best Single Poem for the long poems Twenty Five Laments for Iraq and The Fox in the National Museum of Wales.

The works of globally renowned poet **Menna Elfyn**, the mother of novelist and musician **Fflur Dafydd**, have been translated into eighteen languages, while Caerphilly's **Jonathan Edwards** won the Costa poetry prize for his humorous collection *My Family and Other Superheroes* in 2015, and Cardiff's **Peter Finch**, a commanding performance poet who continues to innovate with his verse and works of non-fiction.

R.S. THOMAS

Deeply spiritual, ferociously nationalistic, and an eternal outsider who had a reputation for being something of an awkward curmudgeon, Ronald Stuart Thomas' (29 March 1913 – 25 September 2000) bleak, brutal, yet life-affirming portrayal of the Welsh landscape and people would establish him as Wales' foremost poet of the second half of the twentieth century.

Born in Cardiff, his father's work as a sailor saw the family relocate to Caergybi, Holyhead, in 1918, and following his mother's wishes, Thomas set out to become a man of the cloth, studying theology at St Michael's College, Llandaff, and ordained as an Anglican priest in the Church of Wales.

It was during the 1940s, while at St Michael's church, Manafon, that his first three poetry collections were published, which formed the basis of 1955's *Song at the Year's Turning*. The collection included a glowing introduction from English poet Sir John Betjeman, who wrote that 'the "name" which has the honour to introduce this fine poet to a wider public will be forgotten long before that of R.S. Thomas'.

Thomas was a staunch defender of the Welsh language, yet wrote more than twenty volumes of poetry exclusively in English, claiming that he learned Welsh too late in life to write verse. Yet he did write two works of prose in Welsh, the autobiography *Neb* (Nobody, 1985) and *Blwyddyn yn Llŷn* (A Year in Llŷn, 1990).

His awards included the Royal Society of Literature's Heinemann Award, the Queen's Gold Medal for Poetry, and he was nominated for the Nobel Prize for Literature in 1996, missing out to his friend Seamus Heaney – who would read the eulogy at Thomas' memorial at Westminster Abbey.

NATIONAL POET OF WALES

Established by Literature Wales, the post of National Poet of Wales, a form of Welsh poet laureate, is a bilingual position in which the chosen poet creates poetry for the purpose of promoting the nation's cultural identity.

Cardiff's **Gwyneth Lewis** became the inaugural poet in 2005, who a year earlier had written the words inscribed on the dome above Wales Millennium Centre, the Welsh line Creu gwir fel gwydr o ffwrnais awen (Creating truth like glass from the furnace of inspiration), and the English line In these stones horizons sing.

Gwyn Thomas, born in Tanygrisiau, Blaenau Ffestiniog, whose words are also inscribed on a Welsh landmark, the Snowdon Summit Visitor Centre Hafod Eryri, took up the post in 2006. Along with his poetry, Thomas' achievements include co-authoring the leading English translation of the *Mabinogion*, the ancient tales which would inspire his three Tir na n-Og Award-winning children's books.

Gillian Clarke, who was born in Cardiff, was National Poet of Wales from 2008 until 2016. A co-founder of the Ty Newydd National Writers' Centre of Wales in Criccieth, Clarke has written extensively for adults and children, and works closely with GCSE and A-Level students who study her words. Clarke's 2012 collection *Ice*, a collection of poems relating to the coming, and going, and coming again of winter, was shortlisted for the T.S. Eliot Prize.

In May 2016, **Ifor ap Glyn** became the fourth National Poet of Wales. Born in London to Welsh parents, the multi-award-winning poet, producer, director and presenter was awarded the crown for his poetry at the National Eisteddfod in 1999 and 2013, and is a multiple BAFTA Cymru winner for his television work.

CHILDREN'S LITERATURE

While there are countless Welsh-language translations of popular children's favourites, from Enid Blyton's *Pump Prysur* (*The Famous Five*) to the adventures of J.K. Rowling's Harri Potter (Harry Potter), the home-grown educational escapades of Sali Mali remain a perennial favourite who, with her friends Jac Do and Jac y Jwc, have helped generations to read, write and count.

T. Llew Jones (Thomas Llewelyn Jones, 1915–2009) from Pentrecwrt, Carmarthenshire, whose career spanned more than fifty years during which he published more than fifty books, has been described as 'the king of children's literature in Wales'. An accomplished poet who won two National Eisteddfod chairs, he thrilled children with the daring historical adventures of the Welsh pirate Bartholomew Roberts and Robin Hood-figure Twm Siôn Cati.

In the English language, some of the world's most cherished children's novels have drawn inspiration from Wales. The title character in **Lewis Carroll's** *Alice's Adventures in Wonderland* (1865) was based on the real-life girl Alice Liddell, who would spend her family holidays in Llandudno – and where Carroll is said to have written part of the book. **Beatrix Potter's** *The Tale of the Flopsy Bunnies* (1909) is set in her secret garden at Gwaenynog Hall, Denbigh, where she would sit and sketch during visits to Uncle Fred in the 1890s. **Philip Pullman**, the author of *His Dark Materials* trilogy which has been adapted for the screen by BBC Cymru Wales, spent the best part of a decade growing up in Llanbedr, with the almost otherworldly North Walian landscapes permeating his work in later life.

THE MAGICAL WORLD OF ROALD DAHL

Dark, grotesque, macabre and surreal – and that's just his children's books.

Roald Dahl (13 September 1916 – 23 November 1990), the wildly imaginative creator of *James and the Giant Peach*, *Charlie and the Chocolate Factory*, *Matilda*, *The Witches*, *The BFG* and *The Twits*, was born in Llandaff, Cardiff, to Norwegian parents who had immigrated to Wales during the 1880s.

While more famous for his comical tales of evil grown-ups and heroic children, Dahl was also an accomplished writer of adult fiction, whose crime stories and supernatural spine-chillers were characterised by their fiendish plot twists and unforeseen endings.

It was his experiences while serving as a fighter pilot in the Royal Air Force during the Second World War that inspired his first published work. English novelist C.S. Forester asked Dahl to write down some of his anecdotes and memories for a story to be rewritten for the *Saturday Evening Post*. But so impressed was he with what he read that he published it, anonymously, as Dahl had written it, entitled *Shot Down Over Libya* (1942) – despite the fact that Dahl was never shot down. It was later reworked as *A Piece of Cake*.

In 1943, Dahl again drew on his experiences in the RAF for *The Gremlins*, his first book for a younger audience, which was written for Walt Disney Productions and intended as an animated film in which the mischievous creatures play havoc with aircraft machinery.

His works continue to provide an inexhaustible supply of stories for filmmakers, from the cult classic *Willy Wonka & the Chocolate Factory* (1971), which was disowned by the author, to Steven Spielberg's big-budget *BFG* (2016), released during Dahl's centenary year. Films for an adult market include *36 Hours* (1956) starring James Garner and based on the short story *Beware of the Dog*, and the Quentin Tarantino-driven anthology *Four Rooms* (1995), which also drew inspiration from Dahl's short stories.

Dahl also contributed to many TV shows, including *Alfred Hitchcock Presents*, *Tales of the Unexpected*, *Jackanory*, and as the host of 1961 supernatural series *Way Out*.

Roald Dahl. (Nationaal Archief)

PUBLICATIONS AND PUBLISHERS

The Welsh Books Council, established in 1961, is a unique national body funded by the Welsh Government to provide services and grants for the improvement of literacy, and to raise the standards of books produced in both English and Welsh.

Literature Wales is a national literature promotion agency with a global outlook, and is responsible for the annual Wales Book of the Year award, festivals at Dinefwr and Tŷ Newydd, and the National Poet of Wales.

The University of Wales Press, established in 1922, is a prominent publisher of academic works, while other Welsh publishers of note include **Gomer, Y Lolfa, Seren, Honno, Graffeg, Firefly** and **Parthian Books**, who publish the impressive **Library of Wales** archive series.

Magazine and journals include **New Welsh Review**, a source of contemporary fiction and articles which emerged from *The Anglo-Welsh Review* in 1988; **Poetry Wales**, a platform for new writing and critical essays founded by Meic Stephens in 1965; and **Planet: The Welsh Internationalist**, which takes an international look at the culture and politics of Wales.

Online sources for Welsh culture news and views include **Arts Scene Wales** and **Wales Arts Review**.

FUNDING THE ARTS

The Arts Council of Wales (Cyngor Celfyddydau Cymru) is the funding and development agency for the arts in Wales.

Principally sponsored by the Welsh Government, the registered charity was established by Royal Charter as the Welsh Arts Council in 1946, changing its name in 1994 after merging with three regional arts associations.

As well as supporting the arts, its responsibilities include the distribution of Lottery funds, to raise the profile of the arts both at home and abroad, to provide advice and information on increasing enjoyment of the arts, and to grow the arts economy in Wales.

LITERARY AWARDS

The **Wales Book of the Year Award** is the country's highest-profile literature award. Launched in 1992 by administrators Literature Wales, awards are given to English and Welsh-language works of fiction, creative non-fiction and poetry.

The Swansea University-backed **International Dylan Thomas Prize**, established in 2006 when it was won by Welsh author Rachel Trezise, is considered to be the world's largest literary prize for young writers, open to anyone under the age of 39 – the age at which Thomas died.

The city also hosts the inspirational **Terry Hetherington Young Writers Award,** which is awarded annually in memory of the Neath-born poet. Open to Welsh or Wales-based writers aged 30 or younger, it is accompanied by the publication of the Cheval anthology from Parthian Books.

The leading award for children's literature is the **Tir na n-Og Award,** founded in 1976 and presented at the Urdd National Eisteddfod by the Welsh Books Council.

3

THE LAND OF SONG

THE BIRTH OF THE LAND OF SONG

While the perception of Wales as a Land of Song is a much-cherished moniker, it was a relatively late invention, coined in the nineteenth century following a boom in religious music, the success of the male voice choirs abroad, and the continued popularity of the eisteddfodau.

Part of the country's innate sense of musicality can, in part, be put down to its innate sense of rivalry. Competition between neighbouring towns fuelled a desire in tight-knit communities, from the pious choristers to the hard-working miners, to produce the best choral singers, the best male voice choirs, and the best brass bands – a conflict which still rages today among some communities.

Conductor Owain Arwel Hughes noted in his autobiography *My Life in Music* (2012) that 'It's impossible to imagine now, but such was the rivalry between choirs, especially in the tight-knit communities of the South Wales valleys, that after competitions, fighting used to break out in the streets'.

Yet Wales' musical traditions can be traced back through the centuries, with bards known to have performed music from at least the time of the first eisteddfod in 1176, with Gerald of Wales noting in 1194's *Descriptio Cambriae* that 'in their musical concerts they do not sing in unison like the inhabitants of other countries, but in many different parts … You will hear as many different parts and voices as there are performers who all at length unite with organic melody.'

TRADITIONAL INSTRUMENTS

Early folk music was performed on a variety of traditional instruments.

A significant string instrument is the crwth, a flat, fretless six-string instrument believed to have roots in the Roman period. Known as a crowd in English, its Welsh name is thought to reflect its bulging appearance. Resembling a swollen violin, the crwth is held in place by a neck strap, and would have been played on the chest with a bow. Surviving examples can be found at St Fagans National History Museum, Cardiff, and the National Library of Wales, Aberystwyth.

Woodwind instruments are known to date from at least the fourteenth century, such as the Welsh bagpipe and the more prevalent pigborn (pipe-horn), a single-reed instrument made from wood or bone and played using finger and thumb holes.

A good source of modern-day recordings of these instruments is the Fflach:tradd record label, with the crwth featuring on Cass Meurig's *Crwth* (2004), and the pigborn on Ceri Rhys Matthews' *Pibddawns* (2007).

THE NATIONAL INSTRUMENT OF WALES

Synonymous with Wales and Welsh music the world over, the harp is considered to be the national instrument of Wales.

The traditional single-row harp, the instrument of choice since at least the eleventh century, gave way to the triple harp in the seventeenth century, an instant hit when it arrived in London from Italy. Quickly adopted by the Welsh, by the eighteenth century it had become known as the Welsh triple harp, and the first Welsh triple harpist is thought to have been Charles II's court harpist Charles Evans.

The position of harpist in the Royal Household continued into the nineteenth century, with John Thomas becoming harpist to Queen Victoria in 1872. Born in Bridgend on St David's Day 1826, Thomas, an eisteddfod-winning harp player by the age of 12, was aided in his education by the patronage of Lord Byron's daughter Ada Lovelace. A prolific composer, Thomas wrote an opera and a symphony, and was given the bardic name Pencerdd Gwalia (Chief of the Welsh Minstrels) at the first National Eisteddfod in 1861.

Thomas' student Nansi Richards, dubbed the Queen of the Harp, followed in her tutor's footsteps when she was appointed at The Prince of Wales's investiture in 1911. Proficient in both the Welsh triple harp and the pedal harp, one of Richards' more unusual contributions to the history of Welsh culture is that she is believed to have been the inspiration for the Kellogg's Corn Flakes cockerel logo, when she suggested to American Will Kellogg that his surname sounded like the Welsh word for cockerel, ceiliog.

The position of Official Harpist to the Prince of Wales was revived by Charles, Prince of Wales, in 2000, and the instrument currently played is a gold leaf harp, which was donated by American-born harpist Victor Salvi in 2006.

Catrin Finch, from Llanon, Ceredigion, was the first of the new-breed of Official Harpists. Having taken to the instrument at an early age, she became the youngest member of the National Youth Orchestra of Great Britain to perform at the Proms at the age of 10, and has recorded with the likes of John Rutter and Julian Lloyd Webber.

Other Official Harpists include Jemima Phillips, Claire Jones, Hannah Stone and Anne Denholm, while harp playing continues to be popularised by the likes of Llio Rhydderch and Robin Huw Bowen.

OSIAN ELLIS

Osian Ellis (b. 8 February 1928) from Ffynnongroew, Flintshire, is one of the country's most celebrated harpists, who has rubbed shoulders with some of the leading musicians of his generation.

A close friend of composer Benjamin Britten, Ellis appeared on many of his first recordings, some of which were written especially for him. As the first harpist to join the Melos Ensemble, he played at the premiere and subsequent recording of Britten's *War Requiem* under the baton of the composer himself.

Portrait of Osian Ellis by David Griffiths.

From folk music to nursery rhymes, Ellis has drawn inspiration from his homeland for his own compositions, utilising the words of Dylan Thomas' *Under Milk Wood* in *A Sunset Poem,* and the myths of King Arthur in *Ymadawiad Arthur* (Morte D'Arthur).

Ellis has been Professor of Harp at the Royal Academy of Music, principal harpist for the London Symphony Orchestra, formed his own Osian Ellis Harp Ensemble, and is the Honorary President of the Wales International Harp Festival.

WELSH CHORAL MUSIC

In the eighteenth century, the Methodist church's disapproval of songs and instruments of a secular nature saw hymns promoted as the music of choice, both as a form of worship and as an acceptable alternative to the popular pastime of drinking alcohol.

Many of the early hymns borrowed heavily from existing English tunes, or were adapted from the frowned-upon folk songs, but they soon developed their own unique characteristics, thanks largely to the inclusion of choral singing in the eisteddfod from 1825, and the ongoing tradition of chapel singing which allowed the congregation to hone their abilities for competitions.

Particularly popular were the cymanfa ganu (singing meeting or gathering) sacred hymn-singing festivals, some of which could last an entire day. The gatherings took on a professional air, with a strict structure, skilled conductors, and four-part hymns written especially for the occasion. Still a focal point for chapel-goers and a regular feature of eisteddfodau today, cymanfa ganu can be found across the world, notably in North America during the North American Festival of Wales.

BREAD OF HEAVEN

William Williams Pantycelyn (11 February 1717 – 11 January 1791), a major figure in eighteenth-century Welsh literature and a driving force in the Methodist revival, became known as Y Pêr Ganiedydd (The Sweet Songster), writing over 800 hymns, the most popular of which can still be heard across the land today.

Born in Llanfair-ar-y-bryn, but raised on Pantycelyn Farm from where he derived his bardic name which translates as Holly Hollow, Williams was a deeply spiritual man who, after hearing the words of Methodist preacher Howell Harris, turned his back on a career as a doctor to ordain as a deacon and to travel the land establishing new congregations.

Two of Williams' more enduring hymns are the English translation of 'Guide Me, O Thou Great Jehovah', and the lyrics to John Hughes' stadium-stirring anthem 'Cwm Rhondda', now better known as 'Bread of Heaven'.

In the Welsh language, the tune of 'Cwm Rhondda' is more commonly sung to the hymn 'Wele'n sefyll rhwng y myrtwydd' (There he stands among the myrtles) by **Ann Griffiths**, Wales' most renowned female hymn writer. Also drawn to the Methodist movement at the end of the eighteenth century, Griffiths spent her entire life in Llanfihangel-yng-Ngwynfa where she composed her verse orally, not as hymns but simply as a way of expressing her own profoundly spiritual thoughts.

MALE VOICE CHOIRS

If there is one sound that has come to define Wales more than any other, it is the rich tenors and booming basses of the male voice choirs which, at the peak of their popularity, would draw crowds of over 10,000 people to watch them compete in the National Eisteddfod.

Having emerged from the working-class heartlands in the 1870s when community music was in decline, the choirs served as a form of recreation for the workforce, fostering unity among co-workers – and a fierce rivalry with their neighbours.

The Morriston Orpheus Choir at Wales Millennium Stadium, 2010.
(*South Wales Evening Post* / Steve Phillips)

When conductor and musician Griffith Rhys Jones, a blacksmith from Trecynon known by his bardic name **Caradog,** led the **South Wales Choral Union** to back-to-back victories at competitions in Crystal Palace, London, in 1872 and 1873, he permanently changed the perception of Welsh music, both at home and abroad.

Assembled from more than 400 singers from across South Wales, the so-called Côr Mawr's (The Great Choir) double victory over the rest of the UK saw Caradog become a national hero, and gave birth to the notion of Wales as a 'Land of Song'. The Thousand Guinea Challenge Cup Trophy awarded to the victors is on loan at St Fagans National History Museum, Cardiff, while a statue of Caradog, designed by Goscombe John in 1920, can be seen at Victoria Square, Aberdare.

In recent times, the decline in chapel attendance has seen many male choirs chose to operate independently of the institutions which once sustained them, and many have opted out of competitions in favour of a more commercial route by broadening their output to include more mainstream songs. The average age of members is also significantly older, attributed to the shorter life expectancy of the nineteenth-century singers, and a lack of uptake from the young. Yet there are still choirs which can trace their history, if not entirely unbroken, back to the nineteenth century, with **Treorchy Male Choir, Pendyrus Choir** and **Rhos Male Voice Choir** still going strong. Other notable choirs include the **Pontarddulais Male Choir,** who emerged from the Pontarddulais Youth Choir after its members became too old to be considered youths anymore, and the renowned **Morriston Orpheus Choir,** who also run the Young Welsh Singer of the Year competition which has helped launch the careers of past winners Bryn Terfel, Leah-Marian Jones and Gary Griffiths.

Cardiff-based **Only Men Aloud** came to national prominence after winning the BBC talent show *Last Choir Standing* in 2008. Formed by conductor Timothy Rhys-Evans, the choir – which originally contained fifteen members but was scaled down to eight in 2013 – have continued to tour, record, and made a memorable appearance at the opening ceremony of London's 2012 Olympic Games.

Rhys-Evans deserves a lot of credit for reigniting a passion for male voice choir singing in the younger generations, establishing the offshoot choirs **Only Boys Aloud** in 2010 – who also achieved game show TV success by finishing third in ITV's *Britain's Got Talent* – and **Only Kids Aloud** in 2012. The **National Youth Choir of Wales,** formed by Tŷ Cerdd in 1984, has also had a significant impact on popularising choral singing with those aged between 16 and 21.

TEN ESSENTIAL MALE VOICE CHOIR SONGS

While all male voice choirs have their own repertoire, which ranges from religious standards to contemporary pop music, here are ten songs that you'd expect most self-respecting choirs to have in their arsenal:

1. 'Aberystwyth / Jesu, Lover of My Soul'
2. 'Ar Lan y Môr' (Beside the Sea)
3. 'Calon Lân' (Pure Heart)
4. 'Cwm Rhondda' (Bread of Heaven)
5. 'Delilah'
6. 'Hen Wlad Fy Nhadau' (Land of My Fathers)
7. 'Men of Harlech'
8. 'Myfanwy'
9. 'Sospan Fach' (Little Saucepan)
10. 'We'll Keep a Welcome'

THE WELSH NATIONAL ANTHEM

Written in 1856 by the father-and-son team of Evan and James James from Pontypridd, 'Hen Wlad Fy Nhadau' (Land of My Fathers) has established itself not only as the national anthem of Wales, but as one of the most inspiring national anthems in the world.

Originally known as 'Glan Rhondda' (Banks of the Rhondda), harpist James had composed the music as a dancing song, with poet Evan later adding the words. After its first public airing at Maesteg's Capel Tabor, now Maesteg Working Men's Club, the now more-familiar title and harmonies were added by John Owen in 1860 who included it in his *Gems of Welsh Melody (1860–64)* collection.

It wasn't long before it became a firm favourite at the National Eisteddfod, and in an age of great Welsh tenors, it was Robert Rees from Dowlais, Merthyr Tydfil – better known by his bardic name Eos Morlais, after the Afon Morlais river – who took the song to the masses when he performed it in Bangor in 1874.

Equally historic was the 1887 National Eisteddfod in London where, for the first time, members of the Royal Family stood for the new anthem, and in 1905 it further cemented itself in the nation's heart when it became the first national anthem to be performed before a sporting match.

Chosen as a counterfoil to the All Black's Haka when Wales faced New Zealand for the first time in a rugby union match, it had the desired effect with Wales winning 3-0 at Cardiff Arms Park.

Despite having three verses, only the first is usually sung before the rousing chorus kicks in. Below are the words to the chorus, with a non-literal English translation:

> *Gwlad, gwlad, pleidiol wyf I'm gwlad*
> (Land, land, I pledge myself to my country)
> *Tra môr yn fur I'r bur hoff bau*
> (While seas secure this land so pure)
> *O bydded i'r hen iaith barhau*
> (O may our old language endure)

A pair of memorial statues to Evan and James by Goscombe John can be found standing in Ynysangharad Park, Pontypridd.

Memorial to Evan and James James in Ynysangharad Park.

O MYFANWY

First published in 1875, no song quite encapsulates the haunting romanticism of Welsh songwriting as **Joseph Parry**'s (21 May 1841 – 17 February 1903) 'Myfanwy', which featured prominently in the film *How Green Was My Valley*, became synonymous with entertainer Ryan Davies in the 1970s, and has since been recorded by the likes of John Cale, Bryn Terfel and Cerys Matthews.

Born in Merthyr Tydfil, Parry's family emigrated to Pennsylvania in 1854, and it was while on the other side of the Atlantic that he developed his love for music and his fervent Welsh, and religious, identity.

The first professor of music at Aberystwyth University, the town would prove to be a fruitful place for Parry, where he was awarded the bardic title of Pencerdd America (Chief Musician of America) at the 1865 National Eisteddfod, and which lent its name to the 1876 hymn 'Aberystwyth', the music of which was later used by South African composer Enoch Sontonga for 'God Bless Africa', now a part of the South African national anthem.

In 1878, with a libretto by Richard Davies, Parry composed Blodwen, the first Welsh-language opera which premiered at the town's Temperance Hall. The three-act opera relates the tale of a wedding in Maelor Castle, during which the soldiers of King Henry of England pay an unwelcome visit.

BRASS BANDS

With its distinct marching rhythm and upbeat tunes, it didn't take long for brass band music to find a home in the tight-knit industrial communities of nineteenth-century Wales. It was actively encouraged by the wealthy employers who were keen for their workers to have a focal point for their free time, and later became closely associated with the Labour movement.

When ironmaster Robert Thompson Crawshay's **Cyfarthfa Band**, formed in Merthyr in 1838, claimed victory at the first Crystal Palace Championship in 1860, it was a source of much national pride, and in the same year brass bands become a regular fixture at the National Eisteddfod.

Wales' most successful brass band are **The Cory Band**, who were established in the Rhondda Valley in 1884 as Ton Temperance before adopting the name of colliery owner Sir Clifford John Cory. Claiming numerous National, British Open and European Champions titles, The Cory Band are believed to be the first brass band to be broadcast on radio in 1923, and have remained committed to innovation, commissioning new works from contemporary Welsh composers including Alun Hoddinott and Karl Jenkins.

Many other current brass bands, such as Cardiff's **Tongwynlais Temperance Band** and Rhondda's **The Parc and Dare Band,** can trace their origins back to the nineteenth century, while the **National Youth Brass Band of Wales** and Anglesey's **Seindorf Beaumaris Band** keep the tradition alive with the young.

ORCHESTRAS

The **BBC National Orchestra of Wales** are Wales' only professional symphony orchestra.

Patronised by the Prince of Wales, the touring orchestra perform regularly across the country and further afield at large-scale events like the BBC Proms, while recording work for broadcast and commercial release, including the anthemic soundtrack to *Doctor Who*.

Having begun life as the Cardiff Station Orchestra in 1928, the orchestra were reinvigorated in 1935 by the BBC, and following a hiatus during the Second World War flourished in 1946 with the appointment of Pontygwaith-born conductor and composer Mansel Thomas to the helm. The following year saw an expansion of its ranks, an increased touring schedule and broadcasting commitments, and the addition of its own chorus.

BBC National Orchestra of Wales at Swansea's Proms in the Park.
(*South Wales Evening Post* / Adrian White)

After several name changes, the BBC National Orchestra of Wales and the BBC National Chorus of Wales as we now know them were established in 1993, and are based in the BBC Hoddinott Hall at Cardiff's Wales Millennium Centre.

With a focus on contemporary music as well as the classics, the orchestra have performed several world premieres, including compositions from Alun Hoddinott and Arvo Pärt. Their commitment to fostering new talent can be seen in their choice of soloists, many of whom have been championed by the BBC Young Musician of the Year biennial competition produced by BBC Cymru Wales, and BBC Radio 3's New Generation Artists scheme, which has aided the careers of Welsh artists such as Wrexham-born pianist Llŷr Williams.

Cardiff is also the home of two prominent chamber orchestras, **The Welsh Sinfonia**, who regularly tour the country with international soloists and also perform newly commissioned works, while **Sinfonia Cymru**, the resident orchestra at Newport's The Riverfront, are an innovative young orchestra who work in partnership with The Royal Welsh College of Music and Drama to provide a platform for emerging musicians.

Founded in 1945, the **National Youth Orchestra of Wales**, considered to be the world's first national youth orchestra, enables over one hundred young musicians aged between 13 and 21 to tour and record, while commissioning new works from the likes of founding member Alun Hoddinott and former member Karl Jenkins.

The country's leading amateur orchestras include **Cardiff Philharmonic Orchestra** and **Wrexham Symphony Orchestra**, while the cutting-edge contemporary arts company **Sinfonia Newydd** premier the works of modern composers from the Royal Welsh College of Music and Drama.

LIKE FATHER, LIKE SON

Having studied with the likes of Ralph Vaughan Williams at the Royal College of Music, **Arwel Hughes** (25 August 1909 – 23 September 1988) began his professional musical career as an organist in Oxford, but it wasn't long before he was back on home soil, conducting new works from some of the country's finest composers as Head of Music for BBC Wales.

Born in the village of Rhosllanerchrugog, his compositions include *Tydi a Roddaist* (1938), a hymn with words by T. Rowland Hughes, *Fantasia for Strings* (1936) and *Legend: Owain Glyndŵr* (1979) for orchestra, and the oratorio *Dewi Sant* (1950), a recording of which, conducted by his son Owain at Swansea's Brangwyn Hall two years after his death, is available from Chandos.

He also composed and conducted two operas for the Welsh National Opera, both of which premiered at Cardiff's Sophia Gardens Pavilion. *Menna* (1953) is a three-act tragedy based on the folk tale of Gwyn and Menna, while the Welsh-language *Serch yw'r Doctor* (Love's the Doctor, 1960) is a comedy with libretto from Saunders Lewis.

While working for the BBC during the Second World War, air raids forced Arwel to constantly relocate, and it was during this time that his son **Owain Arwel Hughes** (21 March 1942) was born in his sister's house in Ton Pentre, Rhondda.

One of the country's most distinguished conductors, Owain has led the likes of the BBC National Orchestra of Wales and the National Youth Orchestra of Wales at home, as well as the Philharmonic Orchestra and the Royal Philharmonic Orchestra. He founded The Welsh Proms in 1986.

GREAT WELSH COMPOSERS

Daniel Jones: Having studied at London's Royal Academy of Music, winning the Mendelssohn Scholarship gave Daniel Jones (1912–1993) the opportunity to travel around Europe where he developed his skills in music and linguistics, later turning to composing in earnest following his time serving in the Intelligence Corps during the Second World War.

Born in Pembroke and raised in Swansea, it was his lifelong friendship with fellow Kardomah Gang member Dylan Thomas which influenced some of his more well-known compositions, including incidental music for *Under Milk Wood* (1954) and his fourth symphony, *In memoriam Dylan Thomas* (1954). He also played his part in Thomas' work, appearing as himself in some of his friend's autobiographical stories, and editing collections of his poetry.

Using his own complex metre system, Jones composed twelve symphonies, along with a thirteenth in memory of the director of the Swansea Festival, *Symphony in Memoriam John Fussell* (1992), eight string quartets, two operas, and chamber, choral and orchestral works.

Alun Hoddinott: A severe case of stage fright put an end to Alun Hoddinott's (1929–2008) early aspirations of becoming a conductor and a violinist, but his intense passion for music couldn't be restrained and would instead lead him to becoming one of Wales' most celebrated composers of the twentieth century.

Born in the Rhymney Valley town of Bargoed, the prolific and ever-evolving composer produced a vast body of work, from his early commissions for the likes of Disney and Hammer Films, to his songs, concertos, ten symphonies and six operas, which included 1999's *Tower*, based on the words of the miners at Hirwaun's Tower Colliery.

A skilled teacher whose pupils at Cardiff's University College included fellow Welsh composers Karl Jenkins and John Metcalf, Hoddinott became a firm favourite of Charles, Prince of Wales, composing music for his sixteenth birthday, his investiture at Caernarvon Castle, and his marriage to Camilla Parker Bowles.

In 2007, the BBC National Orchestra of Wales announced that their new concert hall at Wales Millennium Centre would be named in his honour. Sadly, Hoddinott passed away in 2008, the year before BBC Hoddinott Hall was unveiled, and the orchestra would premiere Hoddinott's final composition *Taliesin* at the Swansea Festival of Music the same year.

William Mathias: William Mathias (1934–1992) from Whitland, Carmarthenshire, started playing piano at the ripe young age of 3, and by the age of 5 was already composing his own music.

The music of the Anglican Church had a profound effect on the budding composer, who became famed for his works of a spiritual nature written for organ and choir, with 1981's *Let the people praise Thee, O God* being broadcast around the world during the royal wedding of the Prince and Princess of Wales.

Mathias' Welsh heritage is evident in many of his compositions, such as a concerto for the most traditional of Welsh instruments, the harp, and in 1980 wrote his only opera for Welsh National Opera, collaborating with writer Iris Murdoch on *The Servants*.

In 1972, Matthias founded St Asaph's North Wales annual International Music Festival, and is buried outside the city's cathedral.

Sir Karl Jenkins: When Karl Jenkins (b. 1944) was honoured in the Queen's 2015 birthday honours list for services to composing and crossing musical genres, he became the first Welsh composer to receive a knighthood.

Sir Karl Jenkins. (*Swansea Life* / Andrew Davies)

The 'Welsh Wizard' from Penclawdd, Gower, was guided from an early age by his choirmaster father, and began his varied musical career as a jazz musician, joining influential progressive rock group Soft Machine in 1972. Later composing advertising music for brands such as Levis and Renault, it was his soundtrack for a De Beers Diamond Jewellers advert which formed the basis for his debut classical recording, *Diamond Music* (1996), which became the first movement of *Palladio*.

But it was *Adiemus: Songs of Sanctuary* (1995), the first in a series of ambitious Adiemus projects, which propelled the much-decorated composer to global fame, defining his distinctive crossover style and introducing his use of imaginary words and sounds for lyrics.

Jenkins has long been championed by radio station Classic FM, a seemingly permanent fixture in their annual Hall of Fame, and has held the title of being the most performed living composer in the world thanks in no small part to his seminal *The Armed Man: A Mass for Peace* (1999), a reflective anti-war composition which saw him invited to New York to conduct the mass on the tenth anniversary of the 9/11 terrorist attacks.

John Metcalf: John Metcalf (b. 1946) wrote his first opera in 1979, but it was his affinity with the words of fellow Swansea-born talent Dylan Thomas which saw him nominated at the International Opera Awards for his seventh opera, *Under Milk Wood: An Opera*, which received its world premiere at Swansea University's Taliesin Arts Centre in 2014.

A varied composer of several major works, including the three orchestral pieces *Paradise Haunts*, *Three Mobiles* and *In Time of Daffodils* which are available on the *In Time of Daffodils* collection, Metcalf founded the Vale of Glamorgan Festival in 1969, and after spending the second half of the 1980s teaching in Canada where he now has dual citizenship, returned to Wales and to the festival as artistic director.

Paul Mealor: Topping the classical music charts is one thing, but few Welsh composers can lay claim to topping the popular music charts as well – and during the fiercely-fought festive week at that.

Born in St Asaph, Denbighshire, Paul Mealor (b. 1975) scored an emphatic Christmas number one single when 'Wherever You Are', written for the Military Wives Choir and choirmaster Gareth Malone in 2011 with all profits donated to military charities, outsold the rest of the top ten combined.

Mealor's 'Ubi Caritas et Amor' was performed at Prince William and Catherine Middleton's wedding in the same year, and debut release for Decca, 'A Tender Light' (2012), spent six weeks at the top of the classical chart.

OPERA

One of the country's most cherished cultural institutions, the award-winning **Welsh National Opera** (WNO) was formed in 1943 when a group of enthusiasts banded together to put on their own operatic productions. Led by Merthyr Vale-born composer and conductor Idloes Owen, they performed their first concerts in 1945, and their first full operatic production, *Cavalleria rusticana*, at Cardiff's Prince of Wales Theatre the following year.

Big changes came about in the 1970s with the introduction of surtitles, the formation of its own permanent Welsh National Opera orchestra who are now regarded as one of the finest in the UK, and the establishment of a professional Chorus of Welsh National Opera, who remain one of the company's major strengths.

Welsh National Opera's *Carmen*. (Jeni Clegg)

The WNO has helped to launch the careers of many home-grown singers, from the tenor Robert Tear who made his debut in their inaugural production, to the Grammy Award-winning soprano Rebecca Evans, who decided to pursue a career in opera following a gentle nudge from her friend Bryn Terfel.

The WNO present three seasons a year – spring, summer and winter – at Wales Millennium Centre, its home since 2004, which consist of a mixture of traditional productions, contemporary works and premieres. These have included the commissioning of Alun Hoddinott's first opera, *The Beach of Falesá* (1974), and the world premiere of Iain Bell's *In Parenthesis* to mark the 100th anniversary of the Battle of the Somme.

Outside of Cardiff, the WNO perform complete operas at Llandudno's Venue Cymru, and tour further afield across England, a fact which is reflected in their funding, with Arts Council England followed by Arts Council of Wales being their two main backers.

Other notable Welsh opera companies include **Music Theatre Wales**, who were founded in 1988 by artistic directors Michael McCarthy and Michael Rafferty. Presenting less well-known and contemporary operas from the likes of Phillip Glass and Michael Nyman, in 2009 they commissioned their first Welsh language production *Stori'r Milwr*, a new spin on Stravinsky's *The Soldier's Tale*.

Mid Wales Opera, founded in 1988 by Keith Darlington and Barbara McGuire, began life as a summer opera school with an annual festival, before taking to the road as a UK touring company.

Swansea City Opera was established in Brecon as Opera Box in 1989 by artistic directors Brendan Wheatley and Bridgett Gill. Initially performing at English Heritage properties, funding from the City and County of Swansea allowed for expansion, with the company introducing a strong focus on education to accompany their performances.

OPRA Cymru are a touring company who perform Welsh-language translations of well-known favourites. Founded in Blaenau Ffestiniog in 2008 by Patrick and Sioned Young, past productions include Rossini's *Barbwr Sefil* (The Barber of Seville) and Donizetti's *Deigryn yn y Dirgel* (The Elixir of Love).

THE QUEEN OF THE OPERA

It might have been Queen Victoria sitting on the throne in the second half of the nineteenth century, but it was the queen of the opera – the so-called queen of hearts – who set tongues wagging, filled newspaper columns and, most importantly for her, packed out the theatre halls across Europe, America and beyond.

Despite being born in Spain to Italian parents before being raised in America, it was Craig-y-Nos Castle in the Swansea Valley that **Adelina Patti** (1843–1919) called home for over half her life.

She became captivated by the area, developing the country house into her own personal castle complete with its own Grade I listed opera house, and with the Welsh people who, while homesick at the end of her last American tour, she described as 'the people who have learned to love me for myself, and not for my voice alone.'

The singer of choice for some of the most powerful people on the planet, President Abraham Lincoln invited Patti to the White House to perform her trademark song, *Home Sweet Home*, and it is said that Queen Victoria herself came out of mourning for Prince Albert just to see what all the fuss was about.

STARS OF THE GOLDEN AGE OF OPERA

Leila Megàne: Wales's leading opera singer of the early twentieth century was Bethesda-born mezzo-soprano Leila Megàne (1891–1960), who began singing from an early age in Pwllheli where her family had settled, and would go on to perform in some of the world's major opera houses.

The National Eisteddfod regular trained in London and Paris, and after a spell performing in France, where she sang for injured soldiers during the First World War, landed a five-year contract at Covent Garden. Megàne married her accompanist and in-demand composer T. Osborne Roberts, helping to raise the profile of many of his compositions such as *Y Nefoedd* and *Cymru annwyl*, and recorded extensively for her time, including the first recording of Elgar's *Sea Pictures* under the baton of the composer himself.

Megàne retired in 1939, and her final concert was at Pwllheli Town Hall in 1945.

Sir Geraint Evans: Having learnt the ropes from WNO founder Idloes Owen, the baritone and bass-baritone Geraint Evans (1922–1992) from Cilfynydd, Rhondda Cynon Taff, performed more than seventy roles in a distinguished career that spanned five decades for which he was knighted in 1969.

The turning point came during the Second World War when, having caught the ear of bass Theo Hermann, he was coached in Hamburg and given an introduction to Covent Garden where he made his professional debut in the minor part of the Nightwatchman in *Die Meistersinger von Nürnberg*.

Quickly emerging as a leading man in such prominent roles as Figaro and Falstaff, Evans appeared in many British premieres, with Britten's Billy Budd written specifically for the singer – a part which he declined due to the uncomfortably high notes, and instead opted for the less-challenging Mr Flint.

Stuart Burrows: Born on William Street in Rhondda's Cilfynydd, the same street as Geraint Evans, tenor Stuart Burrows (b. 1933) embraced the two true loves of any proud Welshman growing up at the time – rugby and song.

But despite looking all set for a career on the pitch, and having been offered a contract with Leeds Rugby League club, he instead opted to follow the musical route, which would lead to him being labelled 'The King of Mozart'.

Making his debut in WNO's 1963 production of *Nabucco*, Burrows was asked by Igor Stravinsky to sing his *Oedipus rex* in Athens, which paved the way to appearances in opera houses around the world, and hosting his own BBC Two series *Stuart Burrows Sings* for eight years from the late 1970s.

Delme Bryn-Jones: Brynamman-born tenor Delme Jones (1934–2001), who added the first part of his birthplace to his name before turning professional, was instrumental in bringing the WNO to the attention of the world in the 1970s with his distinguished performances of Macbeth and Rigoletto.

A Verdi specialist who had spent time working down the mine and had worn the Welsh rugby shirt for the Under 21 team, Jones studied at the Guildhall School of Music and Drama and Vienna Music Academy, making his debut at Sadler's Wells Theatre in 1959.

He quickly rose to the top in a globe-spanning career on stage, as well as on radio and television, which included his own Welsh-language self-titled series *Delme*.

Dame Gwyneth Jones: Dramatic soprano Gwyneth Jones (b. 1936) performed at New York's Metropolitan Opera House ninety-three times, and is as much admired for her stage presence and acting abilities as her singing, which is perfectly suited to the heavier demands of the works of Wagner.

Hailing from the Pontypool suburb of Pontnewynydd, Jones became renowned for the role of Brünnhilde in the *Ring Cycle* at Germany's Bayreuth Festival, returning every year from 1975 to 1980, which included appearing on the Grammy Award-winning recording.

Her close association with the composer continues, taking the role of Isolde in the *Wagner* television series starring Richard Burton, and as the president of the Wagner Society of Great Britain.

In 2012, Jones appeared in Dustin Hoffman's directorial debut *Quartet* as a retired opera singer.

Gwynne Howell: Leaving it until relatively late in life to pursue a career in opera, bass Gwynne Howell (b. 1938) from Gorseinon made his debut at the age of 30 at Covent Garden's Royal Opera House, and hasn't looked back since.

Noted for his diction, Howell has worked continuously at the highest level across the world, performing some of the more demanding roles in the Verdi and Wagner repertoire. His contemporary opera appearances with the WNO include a staging of Peter Maxwell Davies' *The Doctor of Myddfai* in 1996, a reimaging of the Welsh legend based on the Lady of the Lake.

Dame Margaret Price: Mozart and Verdi specialist Margaret Price (1941–2011) began singing as a mezzo-soprano, but it was as a lyric soprano that she became known as one of the biggest opera stars of her generation.

Born in Blackwood, Caerphilly, life was far from easy to begin with, and having been born with deformed legs Price underwent an operation at the age of 4 to relieve the pain.

It was while at Trinity College that she performed on the soundtrack of Charlton Heston's big screen adventure film *El Cid* (1961), before making her operatic debut in WNO's production of *The Marriage of Figaro* a year later.

That same opera would later establish her as an overnight sensation when, working as an understudy for the Royal Opera House, she stepped in at the last minute to replace Teresa Berganza to a rapturous reception.

Price took her talents to Germany in 1971 where she remained until her retirement, returning to her homeland in later years where she switched her attentions from singing to breeding golden retrievers in Ceibwr Bay. While there she was convinced by the local vicar to sing in a Remembrance Day concert at the village church, an ill-fated experience she described as 'the most nerve-racking occasion of my life' and vowed never to sing in public again – she remained true to her word.

Dennis O'Neill: Having been introduced to the world of operatic singing at the National Eisteddfod, tenor Dennis O'Neill (b. 1948) from Pontarddulais initially learned the ropes in Scotland before establishing himself as a leading Italian specialist, in particular in the lead roles of Verdi.

In the 1980s, O'Neill presented two self-titled television series, *Dennis O'Neill* and *Dennis O'Neill and Friends*, and reached the top of the classical charts with the accompanying soundtrack release.

O'Neill has worked tirelessly to help develop the careers of young singers, and became the director of the Wales International Academy of Voice in 2007.

THE WELSH KING OF OPERA

Few singers have achieved such global recognition, or done more to raise the profile of their homeland, than the fiercely patriotic bass-baritone **Bryn Terfel (Jones)** (b. 9 November 1965).

Wales' greatest opera singer of modern times was born and raised on Fferm Nant Cyll Ucha, just outside Pant Glas, Gwynedd, where the son of a farmer began singing traditional Welsh-language songs and performing in eisteddfodau from an early age.

He rose to national prominence as the first Welsh singer to win an award at the BBC Cardiff Singer of the World Competition, claiming the inaugural Lieder Prize in 1989 before taking his operatic bow in the WNO's production of *Così fan tutte* a year later.

Quickly gaining a reputation as an opera singer of considerable talent, in particular with the works of Mozart, Terfel performed across the world, from New York's Metropolitan Opera House to Milan's La Scala, and as his career developed he become synonymous with the operas of another German composer, the more mature and demanding roles of Wagner, notably as Wotan, chief of the gods in the epic *Ring Cycle*.

A Grammy, Gramophone Award and Classical Brit Award-winner, Terfel's heart has never been far from North Wales, and his love for his native tongue is evident, reflected in his Welsh-language recordings and regular appearances on Welsh-language television.

Bryn Terfel. (*South Wales Evening Post* / Adrian White)

He founded the Faenol Festival, or Bryn-fest as it has affectionately became known, on the Faenol Estate in 2000, and was instrumental in launching the Wales Millennium Centre as the creative director of its three-day opening weekend gala, a venue for which he is now an ambassador and where he celebrated his fiftieth birthday in Wales with a concert performance of *Tosca*.

GO COMPARE!

While there's no denying that starring as the memorable, if infuriating, tenor Gio Compario in the GoCompare.com insurance adverts helped raise his profile, Carmarthen's **Wynne Evans** (b. 1972) has since developed into one of the country's most cherished personalities – as much for his character and banter as his singing voice.

An accomplished tenor with a longstanding association with the likes of WNO and BBC NOW, performing is something of a family affair for the singer, whose mother Elizabeth Evans founded The Carmarthen Youth Opera and the town's iconic Lyric Theatre, with his baritone brother Mark Llewellyn Evans also a professional singer.

THE THREE (WELSH) TENORS

Three successful tenors in their own right, **Aled Hall, Rhys Meirion** and **Aled Wyn Davies** are collectively known as Tri Tenor Cymru (The Three Welsh Tenors), a trio of singers who perform a range of operatic and musical favourites along with Welsh-language hymns and folk tunes.

Carmarthen-born character tenor Hall has combined an international opera and concert-singing career with his likeable personality to develop a reputation as a good-humoured Welsh-language television favourite.

Meirion, from Blaenau Ffestiniog, Gwynedd, a former company principal at English National Opera and the first artist to record at Caernarfon's Galeri, was nominated for a Classical Brit Award in 2006 for *Benedictus*, a collaboration with Bryn Terfel.

Davies, from Llanbrynmair, Powys, who replaced original member **Alun Rhys-Jenkins**, is something of a National Eisteddfod expert, receiving the David Ellis Memorial Prize in 2006, having won the Tenor Solo over-25 category three years in a row.

SINGING WITH THE STARS

Mezzo-soprano **Katherine Jenkins** (b. 29 June 1980) is one of the country's most successful, and most instantly recognisable singers, topping the UK Classical Album Chart at almost every time of asking, and never far from the tabloids and glossy magazines.

Born and raised in Neath, the classical-crossover singer, whose international profile was further bolstered by finishing second in America's *Dancing with the Stars* series in 2012, remains loyal to her roots and regularly pops back home to support the charitable causes close to her heart, such as the restoration of St David's church, her family's church where she began her singing career.

The official mascot for the Welsh rugby team in 2005, Jenkins sang the national anthem ahead of the boys in red's famous 11-9 victory against England in the Six Nations, as well as claiming the first of two back-to-back Album of the Year awards at the Classic Brit Awards in the same year.

THE VOICE OF AN ANGEL

Classical-crossover singer Charlotte Maria Reed (b. 21 February 1986) from Llandaff, Cardiff, who would take the surname of her adoptive father and become known as **Charlotte Church**, received her big break in the most unlikely of places – over the phone on long-running ITV daytime show *This Morning*.

After singing Andrew Lloyd Webber's 'Pie Jesu' down the telephone line and into the homes of millions of viewers, followed in quick succession by an appearance on the station's *The Big Big Talent Show*, the Voice of an Angel was born.

Church became the youngest artist to top the British classical-crossover charts, and would go on to sell over 10 million albums worldwide, being a particular hit in America where she performed for President Bill Clinton, and contributed the track 'All Love Can Be' to Ron Howard's multiple Academy Award-winning movie *A Beautiful Mind*.

In 2005, Church turned her attentions to TV and pop music, with her highest charting single 'Crazy Chick' reaching number two, and hosting her own *The Charlotte Church Show* for C4 between 2006 and 2008, for which she was named the Best Female Comedy Newcomer at the British Comedy Awards.

Katherine Jenkins. (David Skinner)

FOLK MUSIC REVIVAL

Spearheaded by patriotic singer-songwriter **Dafydd Iwan**, Welsh folk music, shunned for centuries following religious disapproval, flourished again in the 1970s.

Along with Huw Jones and the financial backing of Brian Morgan Edwards, Iwan's formation of the **Sain records label** in 1969 proved to be a pivotal moment in the folk music renaissance. It provided a platform for Welsh artists with similar sounds and political viewpoints to reach a wider audience, and later for Welsh music as a whole by releasing music from the likes of The Alarm and Bryn Terfel.

During this period, the traditional group **Ar Log** (For Hire) were assembled by the Welsh Committee for the annual French Celtic music festival Inter-Celtic Festival of Lorient in 1976. And despite only intended to be a one-off collaboration, it was there that they met The Dubliners who advised them to stick together, and through various personnel and instrument changes, the group celebrated forty years in the business in 2016.

Canolfan Ty Siamas, the National Centre for Welsh Folk Music, opened at Neuadd Idris, Dolgellau, in 2007, an arts centre and museum named after local musician Elis Siôn Siamas, who – according to the notoriously fanciful Iolo Morgannwg – was the first musician to build a Welsh triple harp in Wales.

Modern musicians continuing the tradition include **Allan Yn Y Fan**, who compose their own tunes in the traditional style and put their own spin on old favourites; Penarth's **Martyn Joseph**, who has been labelled 'the Welsh Springsteen'; and the bilingual singer-songwriters **Cate Le Bon** and **Georgia Ruth** who have developed their own contemporary yet distinctively Welsh folk sounds.

Dafydd Iwan: When Dafydd Iwan (b. 24 August 1943) penned the satirical folk song 'Carlo' – Welsh for Charlie – at the time of the Prince of Wales' investiture in 1969, there could be little doubt where his political allegiances lie.

Born in Brynaman, Carmarthenshire and raised in Bala, Welsh nationalism was ingrained in the singer-songwriter from an early age, who was imprisoned for fighting for the rights of the Welsh language in 1970, and later became president of Plaid Cymru (2003–2010), the nationalist party which his grandfather Fred Jones was a founding member of.

Dafydd Iwan performs at the Llanelli National
Eisteddfod, 2014. (*South Wales Evening Post*)

Iwan began his musical career by translating well-known English-language songs from the likes of Bob Dylan before composing his own music, and while Welsh politics remained an important subject, his romantic songs are also held in high regard.

Iwan's most enduring song has proven to be 1981's 'Yma O Hyd' (Still Here), which he described as 'a celebration of the Welsh nation'. A firm favourite, it can be heard bellowed out on the terraces at sporting events by Welsh and non-Welsh speaking fans alike.

Meic Stevens: Folk pioneer Meic Stevens (b. 13 March 1942), dubbed by some as the 'Welsh Bob Dylan' (which, while being high praise indeed, possibly overlooks some of his other achievements) would prove to be a formative influence on the Welsh folk music revival.

The singer-songwriter from Solva, Pembrokeshire, made brief forays into English language music while living the bohemian lifestyle in London with the likes of Syd Barrett and Captain Beefheart in the 1960s, but following his 1970 album *Outlander* for Warner Bros he returned home and made a conscious decision to try and establish a popular national sound.

It was only natural that he should cross paths with Sain, producing their first EP, 1969's *Dwr* by Huw Jones, and recording his own compositions for the label which remain some of his more popular songs, including the infectious crowd pleaser 'Y Brawd Houdini' (The Brother Houdini).

Along with writing Welsh music classics such as 'Ysbryd Solva' (Spirit of Solva) and 'Cân Walter' (Walter's Song), his many achievements include releasing two EPs with Heather Jones and Geraint Jarman as the trio Y Bara Menyn (Bread and Butter), composing the pop opera *Mwg* (Smoke) with Jarman which was broadcast by Harlech TV on St David's Day 1970, and supplying the theme tune to the BBC's Welsh equivalent to *Top of the Pops*, *Disc A Dawn*.

OGGY OGGY OGGY (OI OI OI!)

Folk singer-songwriter **Maxwell Boyce** (b. 27 September 1943), who can also list comedian, presenter, and all-round entertainer on his CV, became one of the country's most recognisable personalities in the 1970s when his success on-stage mirrored the heroics of the national rugby team that he sang about.

Max Boyce performing at Swansea's Liberty Stadium, 2011.
(*South Wales Evening Post*)

A boy from Glynneath who had worked down the mine, Boyce came to the attention of EMI following his debut album *Boyce in Session*, which was recorded live at Pontardawe's Valley Folk Club in 1971. His first release for the major label, *Live at Treorchy*, which was recorded in front of a live audience at Treorchy Rugby Club where tickets were given away for free to ensure a full house, would go gold and establish Boyce as a national star, with follow-up *We All Had Doctors' Papers* becoming the first – and only – comedy record to reach number one in the British album charts.

Boyce's most well-known composition, the anthemic 'Hymns and Arias' (1971), was quickly picked up by rugby and later football supporters, in particular Swansea City AFC. After becoming the first Welsh football team to reach the Barclays Premier League in 2011, the Swans fans sang their theme tune to a global audience thanks to the worldwide coverage of the division, and Boyce himself performed a new version of the hit ahead of their first home game in the league against Wigan – the first Premier League game to be played outside of England.

ALL THAT JAZZ

While Wales can't lay claim to having a jazz heritage to rival some of its other musical traditions, jazz clubs and festivals can be found across the country, along with the annual highlight, the Brecon Jazz Festival.

Arguably the most famous jazz musician to emerge from Wales is Newcastle Emlyn's **Dill Jones** (1923–1984). Exposed to the Big Apple's thriving jazz scene while working as a pianist on board a ship, he emigrated to New York soon afterwards, forming the Dill Jones Quartet, and performing with some of the biggest names on the scene including Gene Krupa and Jimmy McPartland.

On home soil, Swansea's **Dave Cottle**, whose Dave Cottle Trio are the resident band at Swansea Jazzland, established the International Jazz Festival in his hometown. One of three musically gifted brothers, bass player **Laurence Cottle** has worked with the likes of Black Sabbath and Karl Jenkins, while keyboardist and saxophonist **Richard Cottle** has recorded with Eric Clapton and Tina Turner.

4

COOL CYMRU

In the wake of the Second World War, Wales, along with the rest of the UK, began to embrace the fresh new sounds that were winging their way across the Atlantic, and it wasn't long before home-grown rock and roll stars started to put their own stamp on these edgy, youthful, American songs.

Ammanford singer **Donald Peers** (1908–1973), a popular entertainer who hosted radio shows and starred in films, entertained the troops while serving as a clerk for the Royal Army Service Corps during the war. He became so synonymous with his trademark tune, 'In a Shady Nook by a Babbling Brook', that its title was written on his memorial tablet in Brighton.

The war proved to be a fruitful period for Briton Ferry-born composer **Harry Parr-Davies** (1914–1955), who composed the rousing patriotic favourite 'Wish Me Luck as You Wave Me Goodbye', along with several songs for the ukulele-playing celebrity George Formby. Parr-Davies had a string of hit shows, although *Jenny Jones*, his 1944 musical set in Wales, would prove to be a failure.

In the popular music charts, **Dorothy Squires** reached number 12 in 1953 with 'I'm Walking Behind You', but Wales would have to wait until 1960 for the first Welshman to score a number one single when one-hit-wonder **Ricky Valance** (b. 1939) went straight to the top of the charts with his debut single 'Tell Laura I Love Her'. Born David Spencer in Ynysddu, Monmouthshire, Valance's cover of the Ray Peterson hit would sell over a million copies – despite the BBC's refusal to play so-called 'teenage tragedy songs', popular Romeo and Juliet-style ballads which usually resulted in one or both of the young lovers meeting a sticky end.

In fact, the 1960s would prove to be a significant decade for Welsh chart-toppers, and while Valance might have been the first Welshman to score a number one, the first Welsh person to reach the top spot – Shirley Bassey – pipped him to the post a year earlier.

DAME SHIRLEY BASSEY

Born to humble origins in Cardiff's Tiger Bay, Shirley Veronica Bassey (b. 8 January 1937) is arguably Wales' most recognisable and successful international female singer, with a career which saw her enter the *Guinness Book of Records* in 2007 for chart hits that have spanned the longest period of time.

Dame Shirley Bassey. (Nationaal Archief)

Having left school at 14, she honed her trade in the local workingmen's clubs and pubs by night, while making ends meet by working in a factory by day. Temporarily putting showbiz on hold after falling pregnant at the age of 16, fame – and notoriety – arrived in 1956 when debut single 'Burn My Candle', inadvertently aided by the BBC's decision to ban the song due to its risqué lyrics, helped foster Bassey's image as a racy sex symbol.

A year later, she broke into the top ten with her own spin on the traditional Jamaican song 'The Banana Boat Song', and in 1959 became the first Welsh artist to land a number one single when 'As I Love You' hit the top spot – and remained there for four weeks.

In 1964, Bassey's first brush with 007 saw the soundtrack album for *Goldfinger* top the American album charts, later completing her Bond trilogy in the 1970s with 'Diamonds are Forever' and 'Moonraker'. In the same decade, she became the only artist in history to score a higher chart position with a cover of a Beatles song than the Fab Four achieved themselves with the title track from 1970 album *Something*.

Despite taking a step back from the limelight in later years, Bassey continues to release occasional records, notably in 1997, the year of her sixtieth birthday, when she featured on the Propellerheads' chart topper 'History Repeating', and in 2015 she teamed up with Blake to release her first Christmas single, 'The Christmas Song'.

SIR TOM JONES

Rarely out of fashion since storming to the top of the singles charts with 'It's Not Unusual' in 1965, Thomas Jones Woodward (b. 7 June 1940) has sold over 100 million records in a remarkable singing career that has spanned decades and genres, and was recognised with a knighthood for his services to music in 2006.

Not bad for the son of a coal miner born at 57 Kingsland Terrace, Treforest in Pontypridd, who began singing after developing a taste for American soul music and, in particular, Elvis Presley, who he later befriended in America.

Having taken his first tentative steps into the music business as the frontman of local group Tommy Scott and the Senators, it wasn't until he was taken under the wing of Gordon Mills that he hit the big time, with his new manager steering his solo career, landing a record deal with Decca, and suggesting the name change to Tom Jones – to cash in on the success of the Academy Award-winning film.

Sir Tom Jones. (*South Wales Evening Post* / John Myers)

Jones' foray into the glitzy world of Las Vegas would make his shows the stuff of legend, characterised by his increasingly sexually-charged performances and uniform of a tight pair of trousers and unbuttoned shirts, which were met in return with a barrage of knickers and even hotel room keys being thrown onto the stage by the over-excited female members of the audience – a ritual which continues to this day.

In 1966, Jones returned to the top of the charts with the first Welsh Christmas number one single, 'Green, Green Grass of Home' – despite having nothing to do with Christmas, or even Wales, being a country song written by Nashville's Curly Putman. 1968's 'Delilah' quickly became a Welsh favourite, sung on the rugby terraces and by male voice choirs, reaching number two in the UK and the top spot in countries across Europe.

It wasn't long before Jones landed his own variety TV series, with *This is Tom Jones* (1969), later renamed simply *Tom Jones*, being broadcast on both sides of the Atlantic with guests including Bob Hope, Stevie Wonder and fellow Welsh singer Mary Hopkin.

Following the boom years, the 1970s would prove to be something of an anti-climax, and by the 1980s Jones had turned his attention to his love of country music which, while creatively accomplished, wasn't troubling the mainstream charts.

But this was all to change when son Mark took over as manager and guided another reinvention, kick-started when his father teamed up with the Art of Noise for an unlikely cover of Prince's 'Kiss' (1988). A decade later, Jones again found chart success through collaboration, with Mousse T's tongue-in-cheek 'Sex Bomb' being the stand-out single on the *Reload* (1999) album, which also produced singles with The Cardigans, Cerys Matthews, Stereophonics and Heather Small.

Jones continues to record and tour, and as one of the original coaches on TV talent show *The Voice* was brought to the attention of a new generation of fans in 2012 – until he was unceremoniously replaced by Boy George in 2015.

THE SWINGING SIXTIES

The Welsh number ones continued throughout the 1960s, with rock'n'rollers **The Spencer Davis Group** scoring a back-to-back double in 1966 with 'Keep on Running' and 'Somebody Help Me'.

Hailing from Bon-y-maen in Swansea, frontman and founder **Spencer Davies** (b. 1939) – who dropped the e from his surname to avoid any potential pronunciation issues – formed the band in 1963 while studying in Birmingham. The original line-up split in 1969, but the multi-instrumentalist and honorary member of Plaid Cymru has continued to perform and record music with numerous line-ups and solo projects.

For **Mary Hopkin** (1950), opportunity really did knock after being spotted on the ITV primetime talent show by sixties icon Twiggy, which brought the young folk singer to the attention of Paul McCartney.

Born and raised in Pontardawe, Hopkin began recording in the Welsh language before becoming one of the first artists to sign for The Beatles' Apple record label, scoring a UK number one with her first single at the age of 18, 1968's sentimental classic 'Those Were the Days'.

Her second single 'Goodbye' (1969), written by McCartney, was, somewhat ironically, only kept from the top spot by The Beatles themselves, and a year later she would again finish in second place while representing the UK in the Eurovision Song Contest with 'Knock Knock, Who's There?' (1970) missing out by four points to Ireland's Dana.

Formed in Cardiff in 1966, the short-lived **Amen Corner** are notable not only for their hits in the late 1960s, but for launching the career of frontman **Andy Fairweather Low** (b. 1948) of Ystrad Mynach, Caerphilly, who would go on to carve out a successful solo career and work with the likes of The Who, Joe Satriani and Eric Clapton.

A jazz and blues-inspired rock act, the band adopted a more commercial sound as they set about conquering the charts, reaching the top spot in 1969 with '(If Paradise Is) Half as Nice'. Despite disbanding in the same year, they still had time to re-enter the top five with the Roy Wood-penned 'Hello Susie', and even made an appearance in Vincent Price horror flick *Scream and Scream Again*.

WALES' TOP TEN OF FIRST NUMBER ONES

1. Shirley Bassey – 'As I Love You' (January 1959)
2. Ricky Valance – 'Tell Laura I Love Her' (August 1960)
3. Shirley Bassey – 'Reach For the Stars/Climb Ev'ry Mountain' (July 1961)
4. Tom Jones – 'It's Not Unusual' (February 1965)
5. Spencer Davis Group – 'Keep on Running' (December 1965)
6. Spencer Davis Group – 'Somebody Help Me' (March 1966)
7. Tom Jones – 'Green, Green Grass of Home' (November 1966)
8. Mary Hopkin – 'Those Were the Days' (September 1968)
9. Amen Corner – '(If Paradise Is) Half As Nice' (January 1969)
10. Dave Edmunds – 'I Hear You Knocking' (November 1970)

THE ALTERNATIVE PRINCE OF WALES

Achieving legendary status as a founding member of The Velvet Underground, John Cale (b. 9 March 1942), the last surviving original member of the New York avant-garde pioneers, was inducted into America's Rock and Roll Hall of Fame in 1996, having co-founded the cult group with frontman Lou Reed in 1965.

Their experimental collaborations provided the band's unique – if, at the time, commercially unsuccessful – sound on their first two albums, *The Velvet Underground & Nico* (1967) and *White Light/ White Heat* (1968), in which Cale, the band's bassist, also provided viola, keyboards, organ and occasional vocals.

Fired in 1968 following a rift with Reed, Cale set out on a successful solo career as a musician, composer and producer who found a particular affinity with the 1970s punk scene, later reuniting with Reed on 1990's *Songs for Drella*, a tribute album to their former manager and album cover artist Andy Warhol, and again briefly as the Velvet Underground in 1993.

1973's *Paris 1919* is considered to be Cale's most accessible solo record, which contains a tip of the hat to Dylan Thomas on the track 'Child's Christmas in Wales'. Later setting the poet's words to music on 1989's *Words for the Dying*, Cale was invited to perform his 'Do Not Go Gentle Into That Good Night' at the Welsh Assembly's opening in 1999.

John Cale. (*South Wales Evening Post* / Adrian White)

Cale's interpretation of Leonard Cohen's 'Hallelujah', which featured in the 2001 film *Shrek*, has since become the version of choice for subsequent covers, and his collaborations with artists, filmmakers and writers saw him represent Wales at Venice Biennale in 2009 with his installation audio-visual work *Dyddiau Du/ Dark Days*.

EUROVISION SONG CONTEST

The United Kingdom has competed in Europe's long-running singing competition since its second year in 1957, with Mary Hopkin becoming the first Welsh singer to represent the country in 1970 and who, along with Michael Ball in 1992, remains Wales' joint most successful competitor, with both finishing in second place.

1970: Mary Hopkin – 'Knock, Knock Who's There?' (second place)
1990: Emma – 'Give a Little Love Back to the World' (sixth place)
1992: Michael Ball – 'One Step Out of Time' (second place)
2002: Jessica Garlick – 'Come Back' (third place)
2004: James Fox – 'Hold On to Our Love' (sixteenth place)
2013: Bonnie Tyler – 'Believe in Me' (nineteenth place)
2016: Joe Woolford (from Ruthin) and Jake Shakeshaft – 'You're Not Alone' (twenty-fourth place)

LET'S ROCK

From glam to progressive, hard to heavy, rock music came to the forefront in the 1970s, and Welsh acts and artists played their part in shaping these new movements.

The Rhondda Valley's **Racing Cars** had a hit with 'They Shoot Horses, Don't They?' in 1976, while Brecon's **Roger Glover** played bass for Deep Purple and Rainbow, Wrexham-born guitarist and singer **Andy Scott** joined glam rock chart-toppers Sweet, and Pontypridd axe-man **Phil 'Wizzö' Campbell** joined Motörhead, the longest-serving member after Lemmy himself.

In 1970, **Dave Edmunds** (b. 1944) had a number one hit – and a Christmas number one at that – with his cover of Smiley Lewis' 'I Hear You Knocking'. A producer as well as a musician, Edmunds began gigging in his native Cardiff, first entering the top five with Welsh trio

Love Sculpture's 'Sabre Dance', a fuzzed-up take on Khachaturian's classical piece of the same name, with a cover of Elvis Costello's 'Girls Talk' (1979) being his second highest charting single.

Cardiff's **Budgie**, who formed in 1967 and fused elements of prog rock with an edgier sound and screeching vocals, became pioneers of the emerging British heavy metal scene, influencing the likes of Iron Maiden and later the Seattle grunge movement, with both Soundgarden and The Melvins namedropping the band. Their songs 'Crash Course in Brain Surgery' and 'Breadfan' were introduced to a new generation of metal fans in the late 1980s when covered by Metallica.

Founded in 1968, psychedelic South Walian rockers **Man** established a hard-core following across Europe and in America where, through continuous line-up changes and role swapping, they toured relentlessly with the likes of Badfinger, Hawkwind and Blue Öyster Cult. Life was never dull for the band, who courted controversy when their song 'Erotica' from debut album *Revelation* (1969) was banned in the UK due to the sound of a female orgasm set to music, while on-the-road antics saw them locked-up for drug offences in Belgium and denied entry back into the UK as suspected terrorists.

If the 1980s was a decade of flamboyance and extravagance, no Welsh band quite epitomised the period as Cardiff glam rockers **Tigertailz**. Loud, colourful, and above all else fun, the group formed in 1983 after an advert was placed in their hometown's Spillers Records, and, after a string of line-up changes, strutted their way into the top 40 with 1990's 'Bezerk'.

BADFINGER

Swansea-born Pete Ham (27 April 1947 – 24 April 1975) is one of Wales's most unassumingly influential and sorely missed rock frontmen – a musical genius whose life was cut tragically short when he took his own life at the age of 27.

Badfinger started life as The Iveys, named after Swansea's Ivey Place, renaming in 1969 after signing for The Beatles' Apple record label. Their association with the Fab Four extended beyond just a name change, with their first hit single 'Come and Get It' (1969) written and produced by Paul McCartney, and 1971's 'Day After Day' produced by George Harrison.

Later signing to Warner Bros Records, the band were dogged by legal wrangles and money problems which were blamed on the questionable financial practices of their business manager Stan Polley.

A penniless Ham, with a new mortgage to pay for and a pregnant wife to support, tried in vain to contact the American-based businessman to claim some of his earnings, but having been informed by telephone that all of his money had vanished, he is said to have visited the pub, drank ten whiskies, and was found the next day hanging in his garage. His daughter was born a month later.

On 19 November 1983, bandmate Tom Evans – who had been drinking with his friend the night before he committed suicide – also ended his life in the same manner.

In recent times, the band's cult status has been reignited thanks to two songs in particular. When 'Without You' was written in 1970 by Ham and Evans, it wasn't even considered good enough to be a single. Yet a year later it became a global chart-topper for Harry Nilsson, a feat which Mariah Carey would repeat in 1994 with her biggest European hit.

A similar fate was in store for the single 'Baby Blue' (1972), which originally failed to enter the top 40 in the UK, but has seen its popularity soar thanks, in part, to its inclusion in Martin Scorsese's Academy Award-winning film *The Departed*, and later as the iconic closing scene music in the final episode of American TV series *Breaking Bad*.

In 2013, a blue plaque was unveiled in Ham's hometown, just outside Swansea's train station, and on the same day music fans from around the world descended on Swansea Grand Theatre for a memorial concert featuring former bandmate Bob Jackson.

ROCKFIELD STUDIOS

The legendary Rockfield Studios, a converted farmhouse which lies just outside the Monmouthshire village of the same name, has recorded some of the biggest rock acts on the planet since it first began in the 1960s, including the best-selling album of the 1990s, Oasis' '(What's the Story) Morning Glory?'

Founded by brothers Kingsley and Charles Ward, with Charles going his own way in the 1980s and establishing Monnow Valley Studios in the old rehearsal studios, Rockfield was unique in being the world's first residential studios which allowed artists to fully immerse themselves in the creative process by staying on site in the countryside, an experience which Robert Plant has credited with launching his solo career following the demise of Led Zeppelin.

The studios' first number one single was Dave Edmunds' 'I Hear You Knocking' (1970), and soon after was recording the leading bands of the 1970s, including Black Sabbath, Judas Priest, Rush and Queen, who recorded 'Bohemian Rhapsody' in the Quadrangle Studio.

PUNK ROCK

As anyone who was seen the now-infamous footage of the Sex Pistols rolling into Caerphilly during their Anarchy Tour in December 1976 will know, punk rock wasn't welcomed with open arms by everyone in Wales – in this case, it was met with the protests of vengeful preachers and shivering carol singers.

Yet the rebellious DIY attitude struck a chord with many of the disillusioned younger generation, and the underground punk scene in Wales has, for the most part, reflected that of Britain as a whole, with the antagonistic political sounds of the 1970s giving way to the more sanitised American skate-punk scene of the 1990s.

Early Welsh-language acts of note include **Y Trwynau Coch** (The Red Noses), who formed in Swansea in 1978 and focused on the poppier, fun side of the genre. They would be followed in 1982 by the more aggressive sounds of hard-gigging John Peel favourites **Anhrefn** (Disorder) from Bangor, whose bassist Rhys Mwyn launched the Recordiau Anhrefn record label for the promotion of similar acts.

Aberteifi's **Datblygu** (Development), formed in the same year and also finding favour with the influential DJ who said that 'this is the band that makes me want to learn the Welsh language', released their first vinyl record on the label in 1987, while Bangor post-punkers **Fflaps** recorded two Peel Sessions, with guitarist and vocalist Ann Matthews later forming Ectogram.

Prominent English-language bands include Bridgend's **The Partisans**, whose 1981 debut single caught the ear of journalist Gary Bushell, who included them on three of his *Oi!* compilation albums. Also at the forefront of the *Oi!* movement were Cardiff's **The Oppressed**, whose anti-fascist stance – and their love for their hometown football team – were central to their lyrics, while Haverfordwest's **Picture Frame Seduction** were early pioneers of the British hardcore scene.

As punk drifted into new wave, Cardiff's **Green Gartside**, who formed **Scritti Politti** in 1977, had a string of top twenty singles in the second half of the 1980s and remains the band's only original member. Fellow Cardiff-based post-punkers and Rough Trade Records labelmates **Young Marble Giants** have been credited as an influence by the likes of Kurt Cobain and Peter Buck, despite only releasing two EPs and one album between 1978 and 1980. **Julian Cope**, the frontman of new wave rebels **The Teardrop Explodes** who had a top ten hit with 'Reward' in 1981, was born in Deri, Monmouthshire, in 1957, and was visiting his grandmother in Aberfan during the mining disaster of 1966.

Wales's leading contribution to the psychobilly genre, a fusion of punk and rockabilly, are **Demented Are Go**, who formed in Penarth around 1982 – a date even the band themselves are unsure of – before relocating to a squat in London.

THE ALARM

In 2004, when snotty young upstarts The Poppy Fields smashed their way into the charts with debut single '45 RPM', little did anyone suspect – least of all the radio DJs promoting the tune – that they had, inadvertently, given political Welsh rockers The Alarm their first hit single since 1987.

The song had been lip-synced by the youthful Welsh band Wayriders, and when the hoax, which formed the basis of 2012 film *Vinyl*, was revealed by frontman **Mike Peters** (b. 25 February 1959), he explained that the image-conscious and ageist nature of the music industry meant that any new releases from The Alarm would have been overlooked otherwise.

Born Michael Leslie Peters in Prestatyn, image and age weren't an issue when the band first hit the charts in 1983 with 'Sixty Eight Guns', their highest charting single from debut album *Declaration*.

Having started life in 1977 as Rhyl-based punk band The Toilets, they renamed and hooked up with U2's agent Ian Wilson, which saw a natural bond develop between the two acts. Bono joined the band on stage, and they supported the Irish rock giants on their American tour in 1983.

Peters unexpectedly, but quite amicably, announced his intention to quit the band live on stage at the Brixton Academy in 1991, but continues to tour and record as a solo artist, with a reformed The Alarm, and with an extensive list of collaborations which include punk rock supergroups Dead Men Walking and The Jack Tars, and fronting Joe Strummer's former band The Mescaleros and Scottish rockers Big Country.

In 2003, Peters established the Love Hope Strength charity to fight cancer and leukaemia with American businessman James Chippendale, having both survived the disease.

THE 1980s

Bonnie Tyler: Having put in the hard graft in the local pubs and clubs, Skewen's Gaynor Hopkins (8 June 1951) – aka Bonnie Tyler – first entered the singles charts in 1976 with 'Lost in France', before storming into the top ten in the 1980s with two of the biggest-selling singles of all time.

Bonnie Tyler in Swansea. (*South Wales Evening Post*)

Featuring her distinctive husky voice, the fortunate side-effect of having her vocal nodules removed early in her career, 'Total Eclipse of the Heart' (1983), from the equally successful fifth album *Faster Than the Speed of Night*, made Tyler the first – and to date, only – Welsh artist to reach the top spot in the American singles chart.

A year later, 'Holding Out For a Hero' (1984), recorded for the soundtrack of dance film *Footloose*, became another of Tyler's defining songs, but it failed to set the charts alight at the first attempt, later reaching number two when re-released in 1985. Written by long-term Meat Loaf collaborator Jim Steinman, the 'Bat Out of Hell' singer later claimed that it was originally intended for him.

Tyler continues to tour and record, and spent ten weeks at the top of the French charts in 2003 when she teamed-up with Kareen Antonn for a bilingual take on 'Turn Around' entitled '*Si demain ...*', and represented the UK in the 2013 Eurovision Song contest with 'Believe in Me', a song which – thankfully – avoided the dreaded nul points by scoring a credible (from a UK perspective) twenty-three points, finishing in nineteenth place out of twenty-six.

Shakin' Stevens: It didn't get much bigger than Shaky in the 1980s.

Cardiff's Michael Barratt (b. 4 March 1948) was the UK's best-selling singles artist of the decade, with platinum-selling albums on the back of number one hits 'This Ole House', 'Green Door', 'Oh Julie' and 1985 festive favourite 'Merry Christmas Everyone' – which was delayed by a year to avoid going head-to-head with Band Aid's 'Do They Know It's Christmas'.

The 'Welsh Elvis', a working-class boy from the Ely estate, turned professional in the 1960s as the singer of Penarth-based rockers Shakin' Stevens and the Sunsets, who supported the Rolling Stones in 1969 and released their debut album *A Legend*, produced by Dave Edmunds, the following year.

Barratt's big break arrived in 1977 when producer Jack Good offered him a leading role in his new West End musical *Elvis!*, and chart success arrived soon after, with the star ending his association with The Sunsets and going solo with his first single, 'Hot Dog' in 1980.

Steve Strange: Flying the New Romantic flag for Wales was the irrepressible Stephen John Harrington (28 May 1959 – 12 February 2015), more widely known as Steve Strange, the larger-than-life frontman for synth-poppers Visage.

Born in Newbridge, Caerphilly, where he witnessed the Sex Pistols' notorious gig in 1976, Harrington soon started arranging gigs of his own, and headed for London where he was employed by punk impresario Malcolm McLaren, and formed The Moors Murderers with the iconic Soo Catwoman.

The band split in 1978, and following a short stint with The Photons – with whom he picked up his Steve Strange nickname – Visage were born. At the same time, Harrington found himself at the heart of the emerging fashion-conscious scene as a nightclub promoter, most notably at Covent Garden's Blitz where his policy was only to admit 'the weird and wonderful', with Mick Jagger among those who were refused entry.

Visage's second single 'Fade to Grey' (1980) became a hit across Europe, bolstered by Harrington's appearance in David Bowie's 'Ashes to Ashes' (1980) video earlier in the year – in 2008, he would appear in the TV series of the same name. Initially splitting in 1985 following the disappointing performance of their third album, Visage were later revived with various line-ups and were actively writing and recording new material when Harrington died of a heart attack in 2015.

The Flying Pickets: Formed in 1982 by Ebbw Vale actor and singer Brian Hibbard (26 November 1946 – 17 June 2012), a group of six theatrical actors with a knack for singing a cappella scored an unlikely Christmas number one in 1983 with their debut single, a cover of Yazoo's 'Only You', which itself had only reached number two a year earlier.

Their distinctive image, epitomised by Hibbard's side-burned Teddy Boy look, gave the illusion of a novelty act, but it was their political activism and support for the striking miners – their name itself being a reference to the ongoing strikes – which set them at odds with their record label, and with the shops that stocked their music.

Hibbard would go on to appear in long-running television series *Coronation Street*, *Emmerdale* and *Pobol y Cwm*, and made a memorable appearance as Karaoke King Dai Rees in the film *Twin Town*.

COOL CYMRU

An unprecedented period in the late 1990s saw Welsh rock music dominate the airwaves like never before.

As the popularity of Britpop waned, a handful of Welsh guitar-based bands, spearheaded by a resurgent **Manic Street Preachers**, suddenly found themselves entering the charts en masse in a cultural movement dubbed Cool Cymru by the indie press.

But before the likes of **Catatonia** and **Stereophonics** were headlining festivals and staring back at us from the front pages of the NME, the alternative music scene had been bubbling away in the background for quite some time.

In 1988, record label Ankst joined fellow independent forerunners Recordiau Anhrefn in publishing the best of Welsh-language music, with experimental cut-and-paste merchants **Llwybr Llaethog** (Milky Way) leading the way in the second half of the 1980s. In the same decade, pioneering electronic band **Underworld** were formed in Cardiff.

In 1994, stoner rock forerunners **Acrimony** from Swansea released their influential debut album *Hymns to the Stone*, while the city of Newport found itself prematurely dubbed 'the new Seattle' thanks to indie bands like **The Cowboy Killers**, **60ft Dolls** and **Novocaine**, who all appeared on Frug! Records' fantastically named compilation *I Was a Teenage Gwent Boy* (1994).

At the poppier end of the scale, **The Darling Buds** and **Helen Love** were chipping away at the indie charts, and by the time **Fierce Panda**'s equally well-named *Dial M for Merthyr* (1997) compilation arrived, which saw future household names appear alongside indie favourites like **Big Leaves**, **Topper** and **Melys**, Welsh rock was already spilling over into the mainstream.

As the scene reached its crescendo, a second wave of Welsh artists with a rockier edge kept the momentum going into the new millennium, from the radio friendly tunes of **Feeder**, **Liberty 37** and comedy rappers **Goldie Lookin' Chain**, to the heavier sounds of **Skindred**, **Funeral for a Friend**, **Bullet for My Valentine**, **The Automatic**, **The Blackout** and **Kids in Glass Houses**.

In the pop world, Cardiff singer-songwriter **Donna Lewis** was denied an American number one when 1996's 'I Love You Always Forever' was held in second place by Los Del Rio's dance-floor filler 'Macarena', while **Lisa Scott-Lee** and **Ian 'H' Watkins**, the Welsh duo in pop quintet Steps, racked up hit after hit between 1997 and 2001, including two number one singles and two number one albums.

Bangor-born singer **Duffy**'s debut *Rockferry* went platinum and was the bestselling album of 2008, spawning five hit singles including the chart-topping 'Mercy', while Marina Lambrini Diamandis – **Marina and the Diamonds** – from Brynmawr, Blaenau Gwent, who was named in second place in the BBC's Sound of 2010, reached the top of the album charts in 2012 with 'Electra Heart'. In 2016, Wales-based singer-songwriter **Amy Wadge** was awarded a Grammy for Song of the Year for co-writing Ed Sheeran's 'Thinking Out Loud'.

When it comes to dance music, Newport's James Hannam, better known as **Culprit 1**, 'The DJ Shadow of Wales', and Penarth's Lincoln Barrett, drum and bass DJ **High Contrast**, have established themselves as national radio favourites, while Caerphilly's **Sian Evans**, singer for electronic trio **Kosheen**, featured on DJ Fresh's number one single 'Louder' (2011).

The place to be: Wales has its fair share of renowned music venues, from the capital's ultra-cool Clwb Ifor Bach to Swansea's sorely missed spit-and-sawdust rock haven The Coach House, but they don't come much more mythical, or with more tales to tell, than Newport's TJ's.

Having opened its doors as a live music venue in 1985 until it was sold at auction in 2011, it served as a launch pad for emerging Welsh talent, with local heroes the 60ft Dolls practically making the place their home. It hosted early gigs from the likes of the Manic Street Preachers, Stereophonics, Goldie Lookin' Chain and Catatonia, who recorded the video for 'Mulder and Scully' at the venue.

Benefiting from its proximity to the Severn Bridge, its atmospheric, cavern-like stage became an essential tour stop for any band in the know, from visiting American punk rock acts Green Day and Descendents, to emerging British acts Oasis and Primal Scream.

Legend has it that Nirvana frontman Kurt Cobain proposed to Courtney Love at the venue following a raucous Hole gig. While many consider this to be an unlikely claim, Cobain did indeed drop by on the night in question to catch his future wife's set – and was even denied entry until he explained who he was, and his reason for being there.

Manic Street Preachers: With their revolutionary brand of post-punk rock and distinctive, androgynous look, the rebellious lyrics and headline-grabbing antics of the Manic Street Preachers were the perfect counterfoil to the shoegazing and dance music that had dominated the late 1980s.

And despite claiming that they would 'split up after selling 16 million copies' of debut album *Generation Terrorists* (1992), the band, who formed in Blackwood in 1986, have continued to reinvent themselves with each subsequent release, from the haunting bleakness of the *Holy Bible* (1994), to the European-flavoured sounds of *Futurology* (2014).

Following the tragic disappearance of guitarist and lyricist Richey Edwards in 1995, singer and guitarist James Dean Bradfield, bassist Nicky Wire and drummer Sean Moore returned as a trio with the

James Dean Bradfield and Nicky Wire of the Manic Street
Preachers. (Liam Reardon / Photographsof.com)

single 'A Design for Life' from 1996's triple platinum-selling album
Everything Must Go, which swept the music awards and established
the Manics as one of the definitive British rock of bands of the 1990s.

1998's follow-up *This Is My Truth Tell Me Yours* saw the band claim
their first number one album, along with their first number one single,
'If You Tolerate This Your Children Will Be Next'.

Catatonia: With the infectious songwriting of guitarist Mark Roberts
and unmistakable vocals of Cerys Matthews, Catatonia were propelled
into the limelight in 1998 when their pop-infused singles 'Mulder and
Scully' and 'Road Rage' broke into the top ten, both of which featured
on their triple platinum-selling second album *International Velvet*.

And while not being a single itself, the album's title track, with
the chorus 'every day when I wake up, I thank the Lord I'm Welsh',
remains one of the band's more enduring lyrics.

Having established their indie credentials with 1996 debut *Way
Beyond Blue*, the band, whose line-up for their breakthrough also
included bassist Paul Jones, drummer Aled Richards and guitarist
Owen Powell, would record four albums in total, disbanding in 2001
following the release of *Paper Scissors Stone*.

Matthews has since carved out a successful, and varied, career as a
solo artist, author, newspaper columnist, radio and television presenter,

co-founder of Flintshire's The Good Life Experience festival, and an all-round flag waver for her homeland, notably in extolling the virtues of Dylan Thomas.

Stereophonics: Three working-class boys from Cwmaman who fused classic rock riffs with catchy lyrics and distinctive gravelly vocals became the first band to be signed to Richard Branson's V2 label, and would go on to produce some of Wales' more memorable guitar music at the turn of the century and into the next.

Originally named Tragic Love Company, singer, songwriter and guitarist Kelly Jones, bass player Richard Jones and drummer Stuart Cable plugged away at the pubs and clubs before renaming themselves Stereophonics – at Cable's suggestion, after a name on a gramophone – ahead of their debut album *Word Gets Around* (1997).

An instant success, it peaked at number six in the charts and spawned hit singles 'Local Boy in the Photograph', 'Word Gets Around', 'More Life in a Tramps Vest', 'A Thousand Trees' and 'Traffic'. Successive releases would see the band cement their position as top ten regulars, but would have to wait until 2005 for 'Dakota' to become their first number one single.

The band's membership has evolved over time, with the most noticeable change being the sacking of founding member Cable in 2003, apparently for lack of commitment. Cable would continue to drum with other bands, including Swansea's Killing for Company, before his untimely death at the age of 40.

The Stereophonics. (Sven-Sebastian Sajak)

The band's links with their homeland have been maintained, memorably collaborating with Tom Jones for a rendition of Randy Newman's 'Mama Told Me Not to Come', and the cheeky 'As Long As We Beat The English', a humorous ditty commissioned – by an Englishman – for BBC Sports Wales ahead of a nail-biting Five Nations clash with the old enemy at Wembley Stadium. Wales would just edge the match – possibly thanks to the song – 32–31.

Super Furry Animals: Wildly experimental yet overloaded with melody, the psychedelic, and bilingual sounds of the Super Furry Animals are some of the more creative and original pop songs to emerge from Wales.

Originally formed in Cardiff in 1993 with Rhys Ifans – yes, the Hollywood actor – very briefly on vocals, the established line-up of frontman Gruff Rhys, Huw Bunford, Guto Pryce, Cian Ciaran and Dafydd Ieuan were named, it is said, after a drunken slogan was printed on T-shirts by Rhys' sister.

Having signed with Welsh label Ankst in 1995, who memorably released their debut EP *Llanfairpwllgwyngyllgogerychwyrndrobwllll-antysiliogogogoch (In Space)*, an attempt to enter the *Guinness Book of Records* for the longest EP title, they were spotted by Alan McGee and signed to Creation Records in the same year.

The band entered the top forty with the catchy single 'God! Show Me Magic' (1996) from debut album *Fuzzy Logic*, and following the release of albums *Radiator* (1997) and *Guerrilla* (1999), parted company with Creation Records to record *Mwng* (2000) for their own Placid Casual label, which became the first Welsh-language album to enter the top twenty.

Some of SFA's more memorable, headline-grabbing antics include blowing their marketing budget on a former army tank which they painted blue and converted into a soundsystem to take to festivals, while in 2001 they had Paul McCartney guest on their song 'Receptacle' – he chewed a piece of celery in time with the music.

The group went on hiatus in 2012, allowing Rhys to embark on a solo career which has included soundtracks, documentaries, and the ambitious *American Interior* (2014) project, an album, film, book and mobile application which tells the tale of the eighteenth-century Welsh explorer John Evans, who mapped the Missouri River after setting off in search of a Welsh tribe of Native Americans.

Gorky's Zygotic Mynci: Possibly the most under-rated band to be swept up in the Cool Cymru movement, Gorky's Zygotic Mynci perfectly encapsulated the exuberance of growing up in West Wales with a wide-eyed innocence to their bilingual lyrics, an ear for a quirky melody, and an eclectic style of music that spanned the genres of indie rock to folk, and Avant-garde to psychedelia.

Formed in Carmarthen in 1991 by school friends Euros Childs, John Lawrence and Richard James, the band's unusual name is said to derive from the words gawky (school slang for dimwit), zygotic (lifted from a biology lesson) and mynci, as the Welsh word for monkey, mwnci, would be pronounced.

Having recorded their first demo while still studying in comprehensive, the band, with the addition of Childs' sister Megan on violin, recorded their debut album *Patio* for Ankst in 1992, which John Cale is said to have described as his favourite album ever, and who would later invite the band to perform in his film *Beautiful Mistake* (2000).

Backed by radio guru John Peel and the indie music press, the band caught the attention of the major labels and signed to Fontana Records, who released their most commercially successful album *Barafundle* in 1997, which included the singles 'Patio Song' and 'Diamond Dew', and the follow-up 'Gorky 5' (1998).

Having undergone various line-up changes, the Gorky's officially disbanded in 2006, with some of the members continuing to record and perform, notably prolific frontman Childs who now churns out infectious pop tunes as a solo artist.

1990s COOL CYMRU MIX TAPE

Want to get a feel for the sounds coming out of Wales in the 1990s? Here are ten songs which, while not necessarily the best songs from each band, represent the sounds of the time:

1. 60ft Dolls – 'Happy Shopper'
2. Gorky's Zygotic Mynci – 'Merched yn Neud Gwallt eu Gilydd'
3. The Manic Street Preachers – 'Motorcycle Emptiness'
4. Helen Love – 'Does your Heart go Boom?'
5. Catatonia – 'International Velvet'
6. Liberty 37 – 'Oh River'
7. Stereophonics – 'Local Boy in the Photograph'
8. Super Furry Animals – 'God! Show Me Magic'
9. The Darling Buds – 'It Makes no Difference'
10. Feeder – 'Yesterday Went Too Soon'

REALITY TELEVISION

In the twenty-first century, Wales has seen its reserve of singing stars bolstered by the popularity of primetime reality TV music competitions. And while fame might be fleeting for many, there are those who have carved out international careers following their appearances on the small screen.

The first series of *Popstars* in 2001 launched Hear'Say's **Noel Sullivan**, now a regular musical theatre performer, to the top of the charts, while *Pop Idol* gave a national platform to **Jessica Garlick** and **Andy Scott-Lee**, brother of Steps singer Lisa.

Contestants from the *X Factor* who have found success outside of the show include West End singer **Lucie Jones** and 2009's youngest contestant **Lloyd Daniels**, while **Rhydian Roberts** remains Wales' most memorable competitor, having finished in second place to victor Leon Jackson in 2007. With his unmistakable shock of peroxide blonde hair and a varied repertoire which ranges from operatic favourites to traditional Welsh songs, the singer from Sennybridge, Powys, has since gone on to top the classical album charts and tours regularly in musical productions.

Connie Fisher shot to prominence after winning Andrew Lloyd Webber's 2006 series *How Do You Solve a Problem Like Maria?* and took to the West End stage as Maria von Trapp in *The Sound of Music*. Having been told by doctors in 2011 that a rare condition meant that she would never be able to sing again, Fisher successfully turned her hand to TV instead, both in front of the camera on shows such as *Songs of Praise*, and behind it as a producer.

Over the Rainbow runner-up **Sophie Evans** might have lost out to Danielle Hope on the series in 2010, but still landed the prize of playing Dorothy in the West End as Tuesday night cover for the winner, and continues to perform as a successful solo singer.

In the third series of *Britain's Got Talent*, Swansea schoolboy **Shaheen Jafargholi** so impressed with his rendition of Michael Jackson's 'Who's Lovin' You' that he was invited to perform the song in Los Angeles for the King of Pop's televised memorial service in 2009, while rapping duo **Bars and Melody**, who reached the semi-finals in 2014, were snapped up by Simon Cowell's Syco Music record label.

In 2015, **Côr Glanaethwy**, a choir of more than 160 singers, reached the live finals of the show and finished in third place. **Ysgol Glanaethwy**, the Bangor-based drama school, had previously come close to winning 2008's *Last Choir Standing*, only held in second place by fellow Welsh contestants **Only Men Aloud!** In 2016, mother and son singing duo Jamie Gilpin and Melanie Bell from Bridgend finished in twelfth place in the final of *Britain's Got Talent*.

Paul Potts: The rags-to-riches story of Paul Potts (13 October 1970) has entered the realms of folklore since his audition for the inaugural series of *Britain's Got Talent* in 2007 went viral around the world.

Seemingly destined for ridicule by a panel of stern-faced adjudicators, the unassuming mobile phone salesman from Port Talbot took his tentative steps onto the stage to sing the theme song of his hero Pavarotti. As a spellbinding rendition of *Nessun Dorma* resonated throughout the auditorium, the jaws of the judges dropped, the crowd went wild, and a legend was born.

Born in Bristol to a Welsh father, Potts relocated to South Wales after meeting his wife-to-be Julie-Ann online, and since winning the series has become one of the steel town's most prominent and vocal supporters, choosing to remain rooted in his adopted hometown despite his success and heaping praise on it in the press at every opportunity.

His life story was told in the film *One Chance* (2013) starring James Corden.

Paul Potts at Margam Castle. (*South Wales Evening Post* / John Myers)

5

THE VISUAL ART
OF A NATION

SCULPTING WALES

From ancient monoliths to reflective war memorials, sculptures past and present can be found across Wales.

The country's oldest sculpture is believed to be a Mesolithic carving called **Venus**, part of Carmarthenshire County Museum's collection which was discovered at Marloes, Pembrokeshire, among the Nab Head horde of shale beads.

Other early objects of note include the imposing prehistoric sandstone Celtic **Hendy Head** at Oriel Ynys Môn which is thought to represent a pagan god, while the **Caergwrle bowl** at National Museum Wales is a Middle Bronze Age item made from shale and decorated with tin and gold resembling a boat decorated with oars, shields and waves.

Christian iconography played an important role in shaping the art of later centuries, with crosses and stone carvings displayed prominently across the land. The only remaining part of a fifteenth-century **Tree of Jesse** at Abergavenny's Priory Church of St Mary, a reclining figure carved from oak, has been described by art historian Andrew Graham-Dixon as the 'only one unarguably great wooden figure' to survive the iconoclasm, which saw works of a religious nature destroyed during the Protestant reformation.

In recent times, prominent examples of modern public art include **Brian Fell**'s enormous Merchant Seafarers' War Memorial outside The Senedd in Cardiff Bay, a double-sided steel sculpture with the face of a merchant on one side, and the hull of a ship on the other.

Sebastien Boyesen, whose Welsh works include Newport's *The Vision of Saint Gwynllyw* and Port Talbot's *Mortal Coil*, designed Abertillery's *Guardian*, a towering 12.6m-tall miner made from steel ribbons with the names of those who lost their lives at the 1960 Six Bells colliery disaster cut into its 7.4m-high plinth.

Outside of Wales, the distinctive hares of **Barry Flanagan** from Prestatyn can be seen across the world, with his bronze animals displayed in cities including London, Washington and Cologne.

THE GREAT WELSH SCULPTORS

John Gibson: Considered to be the finest marble carver of his time, John Gibson (19 June 1790 – 27 January 1866) from Gyffin, Conwy, was a neoclassical sculptor who reintroduced the practice of tinting marble in the ancient Greek tradition.

After his family relocated to Liverpool, a young Gibson caught the eye of William Roscoe while apprenticing for a pair of monumental masons, and it was the patronage of the historian that led to him submitting his work to the Royal Academy.

So impressed was sculptor John Flaxman that he convinced Gibson to visit Italy, where he flourished under the guidance of leading neoclassicist Antonio Canova, and drew inspiration from the everyday Italian people which he combined with classical Greek themes for his work.

A Royal Academician, Gibson's *Phaeton driving the Chariot of the Sun*, a superb example of his bas-relief, is part of the collection at National Museum Cardiff, and his portrait, along with some of his sculptures, can be seen at Rhyl's Bodelwyddan Castle.

Sir William Goscombe John: Goscombe John (21 February 1860 – 15 December 1952) set out to depict a more true-to-life representation of the human body in sculpture, and in so doing established himself on the international stage as a leading figure in the New Sculpture movement, and at the forefront of a Welsh cultural flourishing during the Edwardian era.

Born in Canton, Cardiff, by the age of 14 he was already assisting his wood carver father in restoring his hometown's castle, before going on to study and settle in London as the assistant of sculptor Thomas Nicholls, who had also worked on Cardiff Castle.

Playing a pivotal part in the culture of his homeland, Goscombe John designed the medals for the National Eisteddfod, along with the *Hirlas Horn* (the Horn of Plenty) in 1898, and the regalia for the Investiture of the Prince of Wales in 1911, which incorporated the Welsh dragon and daffodil symbols.

As a founding member of the National Museum of Wales, he designed the *Trowel, Mallet and Spirit Level* with which King George V laid its foundations, the *Seal* for its official opening, and greatly enhanced its collection with a donation of his own work.

In 1916, David Lloyd George unveiled Cardiff City Hall's Marble Hall, a collection of ten iconic Welsh historical figures, at the centre of which stands Goscombe John's *Saint David*.

Goscombe John is probably best known now for his war memorials, notably those standing in Newcastle-upon-Tyne, London's St Paul's Cathedral and Merseyside, while memorials on Welsh soil can be found in Lampeter, Penarth, Llandaff, Bodhyfryd, Llanelli and Carmarthen.

John Evan Thomas: While a lot of Brecon-born sculptor John Evan Thomas' (15 January 1810 – 9 October 1873) work is now lost to time, his *Death of Tewdrig*, which depicts the final moments of the King of Gwent, survives as two casts which can be seen at Brecknock Museum and National Museum Wales.

The iconic sculpture, in which a sword-wielding Tewdrig Mawr, having defeated the Saxons, is flanked by his daughter and a harp-playing bard, was created for the Abergavenny Eisteddfod in 1848 following a suggestion from patron Lady Llanover, and was later shown at the Royal Academy in 1849 and The Great Exhibition in 1851.

Having learned his trade from Sir Francis Leggatt Chantrey, Thomas began his career by creating Welsh church monuments in the 1830s before specialising in portraits in London, where one of his more notable statues, the *Second Marquess of Londonderry*, can be found outside Westminster Abbey.

Examples of his work in Wales include a memorial to Albert, the Prince Consort, which stands tall on Tenby's Castle Hill, a statue of Cardiff's Second Marquess of Bute in Cardiff's city centre, with likenesses of John Henry Vivian in Swansea, Sir Charles Morgan in Newport, and the Duke of Wellington and other statues at his hometown's cathedral.

The Death of Tewdrig cover illustration from *The People's Illustrated Journal*, 1852.

CERAMICS

In the nineteenth century, Wales developed a proud reputation for the quality and commerciality of the ceramics that it produced.

Swansea-based **Cambrian Pottery**, established in 1764 by William Coles, became a market leader by emulating the model established by Staffordshire's Josiah Wedgwood, and employed many leading artists, including renowned enameller Thomas Pardoe.

The collectable Swansea china and porcelain for which the city become famous, a collection of which can be seen at Swansea Museum, was created with potter Lewis Weston Dillwyn at the helm, who would later offer his facilities to the then-struggling William Billingsley of **Nantgarw Pottery**.

Billingsley, who created some of the most sought after items made in Wales, founded Nantgarw Pottery in 1813 in Nantgarw House just outside Cardiff with his son-in-law Samuel Walker, who would himself open the Temperance Hill Pottery with his wife in New York.

Other Swansea-based potteries of the period include the smaller-scale **Glamorgan Pottery** and **Callands Pottery** in Landore.

THE WORLD OF GROGGS

Groggs creator John Hughes in the 1970s. (World of Groggs)

From Gareth Edwards to Tom Jones, as a Welsh personality it's not getting knighted that means you've hit the big time – it's getting 'grogged'.

The art of creating ceramic caricatures of well-known Welsh personalities began in 1965 when John Hughes (1935–2013) experimented with making mythological creatures and so-called Uglies out of clay in his garden shed in Treforest, south-east of Pontypridd, with the name Groggs derived from the clay used to make them.

The popularity of the Groggs that resembled the rugby players of the time was bolstered by the on-pitch heroics of the national team, and by 1971 Hughes was the proprietor of his very own Groggshop in the nearby Dan-y-Graig pub, which is now maintained by his family who continue to produce the highly collectible figures.

THE GREAT LANDSCAPE PAINTERS

In the eighteenth century, Wales firmly established itself in the world of painting, with Richard Wilson – arguably the most important Welsh painter of all – emerging as a pioneer of landscape painting. The untamed wilderness of the land served as a magnet for a growing crop of romantic tourists, and British painters found themselves drawn across the border for inspiration, thanks in part to the publication of illustrated books which brought the previously unseen rugged beauty of the country to the attention of the rest of the UK, and also aided by the outbreak of the French Revolution, which made traditional European destinations of choice inaccessible.

Possibly the most famous landscape painter of all, **J.M.W. Turner**, toured Wales extensively to sketch the castles and scenery that he would later paint in his studio, and it was on his first tour at the age of 17 in 1792 that he made detailed drawings of Tintern Abbey.

In 1789, painter **Julius Caesar Ibbotson** visited Viscount Mount Stuart in Cardiff Castle, and would remain in Wales for years to document everyday life, from dramatic scenes of the Industrial Revolution to gentler moments of working people and their livestock. Other artists making their way across the country at the time included **John Sell Cotman, David Cox, Francis Towne**, and leading caricaturist **Thomas Rowlandson**.

THE FATHER OF
BRITISH LANDSCAPE PAINTING

Dubbed the father of British landscape painting by eminent art critic John Riskin, **Richard Wilson** (1 August 1714 – 15 May 1782), who would influence the likes of John Constable and J.M.W. Turner, played a major role in establishing the concept of painting the land purely for aesthetic reasons.

The son of a clergyman from Penegoes, Montgomeryshire, Wilson honed his craft in London as a portrait painter, but it was during a formative visit to Italy in 1750 that he turned his attention to landscapes, with Rome inspiring his iconic *St Peter's and the Vatican from the Janiculum* (*c*.1753).

Back in London, his unique combination of the grand style and classical themes mixed with the harsher elements of the natural world was epitomised in *The Destruction of the Children of Niobe* (1760), which brought widespread acclaim and a series of commissions.

His Welsh subjects included the castles of Caernarfon, Cilgerran, Conwy, Dinas Bran, Dolbadarn and Pembroke, the mountains of Snowdonia, and the river at Penegoes from his hometown which, along with many other works, and his portrait by Anton Raphael Mengs, can be found in the collection of National Museum Cardiff.

One of thirty-four founding members of London's Royal Academy of Arts, ill health forced Wilson home to Wales in 1781, where he died a year later and is buried in St Mary's church, Mold.

THE BARD'S LAST STAND

A pupil of Richard Wilson, **Thomas Jones** (26 September 1742 – 29 April 1803) followed in his mentor's footsteps by painting the striking landscapes of Italy and his homeland, and is best remembered today for creating one of Wales' most iconic paintings, 1774's *The Bard*.

Based on Thomas Gray's influential Celtic revival poem The Bard. A Pindaric Ode (1757), the scene is set on Snowdonia where the last surviving Welsh bard, dressed in a flowing druidic robe and clutching a harp, defiantly prepares to jump to his death after placing a curse on the invading army of Edward I.

Also known as Thomas Jones of Pencerrig after his father's estate in Llanelwedd, it was his family's wish for Jones to enter the Church, but compelled to follow an artistic path he instead opted to study life drawing in London's St Martin's Lane Academy.

Wracked by doubt in his ability to capture the human form, he instead turned his attentions to landscape painting under the tutelage of Wilson, and collaborated with English painter John Hamilton Mortimer, who would provide the human figures for his grand landscapes.

In later life, his father's inheritance would see Jones drawn back to his native Pencerrig, his affection for which he wrote about in the poem Petraeia (1791) where, as the wealthy owner of an estate, he lost interest in painting. Jones is buried in his family's chapel at Caebach, Llandrindod Wells.

While Jones achieved success in his lifetime, it was only after his death that a series of convention-breaking personal paintings were unearthed, such as the National Gallery's *A Wall in Naples* (1782), which have since became recognised as a precursor to the plein-air paintings later popularised by the Impressionists.

ART SCHOOLS AND ACADEMIES

Traditionally, Welsh artists would gravitate to England for work and training, but things began to change in the second half of the nineteenth century with the emergence of local art schools, and the establishment of the country's first colleges for fine art, with **Swansea College of Art** founded in 1853, and **Cardiff School of Art and Design** in 1865.

Prior to that, the Snowdonia village of Betws-y-Coed hosted what has been described as the 'first artists' colony in Britain', where **David Cox**, who first visited in 1844, would spend his summers in the Royal Oak Hotel, hosting fellow painters who joined him in Wales.

One such painter was **Henry Clarence Whaite** who, in 1881, would prove to be instrumental in founding the **Royal Cambrian Academy of Art**. Originally known as the Cambrian Academy of Art until Queen Victoria gave it the royal seal of approval, the academy's first exhibition was held in Llandudno before settling at the Elizabethan mansion house Plas Mawr, later moving to Crown Lane, Conwy, in 1993. Its presidents have included Augustus John and Kyffin Williams.

While the Royal Cambrian Academy of Art grew in the north, there was a perceived neglect from artists in the south who, in 1948, formed their own South Wales Group. Renaming itself the **Welsh Group** in 1975 to reflect the now entirely professional collective's expansion into the north, and across the border and into South West England, its members have included Brenda Chamberlain, Arthur Giardelli and Tony Goble.

One of the more innovative Welsh art groups to emerge during the twentieth century were **56 Group Wales** (Grŵp 56 Cymru), formed by twelve disillusioned members of the South Wales Group in 1956. With a modernist outlook, the group continues to promote and display contemporary art across Wales and further afield.

THE DEVIL IS IN THE DETAIL

One of the most well-known – and controversial, due to its apparent heretical connotations – pieces of Welsh art is *Salem*, painted by **Sydney Curnow Vosper** in 1908 and housed in the Lady Lever Art Gallery, Port Sunlight, Wirral.

On the face of it, it appears harmless enough; a romanticised image of a church congregation at the turn of the century with Siân Owen, a homely Welsh woman garbed in traditional Welsh dress, serving as its focal point.

Having been exhibited at the Royal Academy in London in 1909, it found mass appeal when Sunlight soap used prints of the painting for promotional purposes, and could soon be found hanging on the walls of countless homes in the form of reprints and calendars.

As a result, the finer details of the painting were scrutinised closer than they might otherwise have been, and a few questions were raised: why is there a ghostly face looking in through the window? And what is its supernatural purpose? Why was Owen, judging by the time on the clock, arriving late for the service? Or even worse for the God-fearing faithful, was she actually leaving early in protest? Why was she vainly clad in a borrowed shawl much more showy that the one she would usually have worn?

And the most remarked upon feature of all: why is the face of the Devil himself lurking in the folds of her shawl? It is claimed that the Devil's features – horns, eyes, nose and beard – are clearly visible in the shawl, and while Vosper denied any intentional hidden meanings, the rumours have only served to add to the painting's enduring popularity and notoriety.

THE PASSION OF THE DAVIES SISTERS

A firm Nonconformist upbringing would instil a sense of Christian responsibility in philanthropists **Gwendoline** (1882–1951) and **Margaret Davies** (1884–1963), who amassed one of the most impressive private art collections in Britain, and had a major impact on the culture of Wales when they donated over 260 pieces from the likes of Renoir, Monet and Rodin to the National Museums and Galleries of Wales.

The sisters were born in Llandinam, Powys, and a sizeable family fortune from their Victorian industrialist grandfather David Davies allowed them to focus their time on works of compassion, which included substantial donations to charity and joining the French Red Cross during the First World War.

It was in their country mansion, Gregynog Hall in Tregynon, that they fostered a vibrant arts community for musicians and artists, and established Gregynog Press, a private press for producing visually appealing publications.

TWENTIETH-CENTURY LANDSCAPES

The untamed Welsh landscapes have remained a vital source of inspiration for artists over the centuries, no more evident than in the works of Wales' leading twentieth-century landscape painter, **Sir John 'Kyffin' Williams** (9 May 1918 – 1 September 2006).

Sir Kyffin Williams in Cardiff's Albany Gallery, 2004.
(*South Wales Evening Post* / John Corbett)

Williams, who took his grandmother's maiden name Kyffin, had been destined for a career as a land agent, but having been denied entry into the army on the eve of the Second World War due to his epilepsy, was instead advised by a doctor that 'As you are, in fact, abnormal, I think it would be a good idea if you took up art'.

He did just that, by studying at Slade School of Fine Art and taking up a teaching job at Highgate School, where he taught the likes of composers John Tavener and John Rutter, alongside developing his own skills, opening his first exhibition in 1948.

By applying his paint with a palette knife, his distinctive style would capture North Wales like never before, in particular his native Anglesey where he joined a fund-raising campaign to establish Oriel Ynys Môn, Anglesey's Centre for Art and History, which now houses the world's largest collection of Williams' paintings in its Oriel Kyffin Williams gallery, alongside the complete collection of wildlife artist Charles Tunnicliffe.

Other twentieth-century landscape painters of note include **Peter Prendergast** (1946–2007) from Abertridwr, Caerphilly, who was considered – some would say unfairly – as Wales's second-best landscape painter of his generation after Williams. Prendergast also drew inspiration from the wilds of North Wales, from the Penrhyn slate quarry to the Snowdonia mountain ranges, and achieved international acclaim, notably in America for his striking paintings of New York.

The paintings of **Gwilym Prichard** (1931–2015), from Llanystumdwy, Gwynedd, are noted for their vivid use of colour, with the town of Tenby proving to be his muse in later life.

THE ARTISTIC SIBLINGS

One was a recluse who found solace in Catholicism, the other an extrovert with a legendary lifestyle – you probably couldn't wish for two more contrasting siblings than **Gwendolen 'Gwen' John** (22 June 1876 – 18 September 1939), born in Haverfordwest, and **Augustus John** (4 January 1878 – 31 October 1961), born in Tenby.

Two of four children, their mother, a budding watercolourist who passed away early in their lives, fostered a love of art in her children, and the pair would go on to study and board together at London's Slade School of Fine Art, which was unique in being the only British art school to accept female artists at the time.

It didn't take long for teacher Henry Tonks to recognise something special in Augustus, who won the Slade Prize for his painting *Moses*

Dylan Thomas' daughter Aeronwy with Augustus John's portrait
of her father, 2003. (*South Wales Evening Post* / John Corbett)

and the Brazen Serpent at the age of 20, with Gwen later claiming the
Melvill Nettleship Prize for Figure Composition.

Augustus, who came to be regarded as the finest British artist of his
time and was compared to the likes of Gauguin and Matisse, was a
bohemian in the true sense of the word. He lived life by his own rules,
from pioneering new techniques of oil sketching, to his eccentric way
of life as a celebrity artist, with a notorious dress sense, a fondness for
a drink, a string of illegitimate children, and a period of touring in a
gypsy caravan during which he established a commune in Dorset.

Gaining a reputation as a portrait artist for the rich and famous, his
subjects included David Lloyd George, Thomas Hardy, James Joyce
and T.E. Lawrence. He painted Dylan Thomas twice, on the second
occasion employing his son to keep the poet supplied with beer to
ensure he remained seated, and introduced him to his mistress – and
Thomas' future wife – Caitlin Macnamara.

While not particularly known for his landscape painting, one of the
more important, if short-lived periods in his career was as a member of
the Arenig school of painters, named after the Arenig Fawr mountain
in Snowdonia. Along with fellow Welshman James Dickson Innes and
Australian Derwent Lees, the group traversed the mountain ranges of
North Wales in search of the perfect painting locations.

Gwen's career, on the other hand, took a wildly different path to that of her brother, and while far from prolific, her painstakingly detailed works of art led to Augustus prophesising that 'In fifty years' time, I will be known as the brother of Gwen John.'

Fresh from their studies at Slade, the pair visited France together, but while Augustus returned to the UK, Gwen grew attached to the country, which allowed her to rub shoulders with the likes of Picasso and Matisse.

It was while in Paris that she began modelling for Auguste Rodin, and struck up an intense ten-year relationship with the renowned sculptor. Described as an unhealthy, obsessive attachment on Gwen's part, it was during this period that she painted her powerful *Self Portrait* (1902), and after the affair with Rodin came to an end, turned to the Church and retired to a life of solitude with her cats and the nuns in Meudon.

Her portraits of the founder of the Dominican Sisters of Charity Mère Marie Poussepin would characterise her later style of producing small-scale, three-quarter-length portraits of unidentified women.

LONDON'S LOSS IS SWANSEA'S GAIN

A major piece of Empirical artwork, both in scale and subject, was commissioned in 1924 by the House of Lords to commemorate the fallen peers who had lost their lives during the First World War.

But the gigantic, eighteen-panel mural does not, as intended, adorn a special wall in the Royal Gallery. Instead, it has pride of place in Swansea's Brangwyn Hall, which was named after its creator, the Anglo-Welsh painter and artist **Sir Frank William Brangwyn** (12 May 1867 – 11 June 1956).

Born in Bruges, Belgium, where his father was designing a parish church, Brangwyn's family returned to the UK when he was 7 years old, and ten years later had his first painting accepted for the Royal Academy Summer Exhibition.

Brangwyn was soon picking up commissions at home and abroad, but it was the First World War that would come to define him as an artist.

He produced more than eighty British propaganda posters for the war effort, one of which, with its graphic depiction of an enemy solider being bayonetted to the tagline 'Put Strength in the Final Blow: Buy War Bonds', is said to have so incensed the Kaiser that he personally put a price on the artist's head.

It was following the conflict that he received the commission to create his most famous work, a multi-mural memorial for the House of Lords in memory of those who had not returned.

But rather than focus on the more sombre aspects of war, such as a battlefield littered with bodies, Brangwyn instead chose to highlight what he saw as the positive outcome of war – successfully defending all that made the British Empire great, with a colourful scene packed with exotic wildlife and luscious foliage.

Those who commissioned the panels agreed, but unfortunately for Brangwyn, they died before he completed his work, and their successors deemed it wholly inappropriate.

The paintings had to find a new home, one that could accommodate such a large collection, and it just so happened that Swansea City Council were in the processes of creating a new hall, the design of which could be tailored to accommodate all sixteen original panels – which they chose to expand to eighteen – and the Brangwyn Hall, as it became known, was inaugurated on 23 October 1934.

THE AWAKENING OF AN ARTIST

Christopher Williams (7 January 1873 – 19 July 1934) drew inspiration from the literature and heritage of his homeland for his patriotic paintings, and as a firm backer of the National Eisteddfod served as an adjudicator and supporter for the next generation of Welsh artists.

Yet despite being a staunch socialist, he also towed the establishment line when needed, actively seeking commissions in London to paint the elite of society, and initiating an invitation from King George V to capture the Investiture of the Prince of Wales at Caernarfon Castle in 1911.

Born in Maesteg at his father's shop, which is now marked by a blue plaque, Williams lost his mother early in life and was raised primarily by his father whose hopes for his son to become a doctor were dashed one fateful day in 1892 when, on a school outing, Williams cast his eyes upon Frederick Leighton's *Perseus and Andromeda* at Liverpool's Walker Art Gallery.

With his course in life now decided on, he began learning his trade in Neath before studying at the Royal College of Art and the Royal Academy Schools, and was soon exhibiting in the Royal Gallery. Gaining a reputation for his portraiture, he was invited to join the Royal Society of British Artists, and would paint three portraits of David Lloyd George, along with the likes of fellow Welshmen Sir John Rhys, Sir Henry Jones and Sir John Morris Jones.

His Welsh-inspired series of paintings include the Mabinogion trilogy of *Ceridwen* (1910), *Branwen* (1915) and *Blodeuwedd* (1937), the iconic *Deffroad Cymru* (The Awakening of Wales, 1911), a powerful depiction of a semi-nude female backed by a fire-breathing red dragon, and the defining Welsh painting of the First World War, *The Welsh at Mametz Wood* (1920), the scene of which Williams visited in 1916.

While Williams' paintings can be found in collections across the country, of special note are the six which he donated to his hometown which are on display at Maesteg Town Hall.

TWENTIETH-CENTURY ARTISTS

Josef Herman: Born in Poland, the Jewish immigrant Josef Herman (1911–2000) – or Joe Bach as he affectionately became known to the locals – developed a strong affinity with the miners of South Wales after arriving in Ystradgynlais for a holiday in 1944.

It would turn out to be a long holiday, with the expressionist painter remaining in the Swansea Valley for eleven years to capture the working classes as they went about their daily lives.

The National Eisteddfod Gold Medal winner considered his *Miners* panel, commissioned for the Festival of Britain national exhibition in 1951, to be his most important piece of work in Wales.

The village of Ystradgynlais established the Josef Herman Art Foundation at its Welfare Hall in 2004, to both commemorate his legacy and to encourage a wider appreciation of the arts through awards, exhibitions and events.

Ceri Richards: A visit to the Davies sisters' vast collection of impressionist paintings at Gregynog Hall would inspire Ceri Richards (1903–1971), then a young student at Swansea College of Art, to go on to become one of Wales' leading international artists, whose varied work can be found in galleries across the world.

Born in Dunvant, Swansea, to deeply religious, Welsh-speaking parents, the influence of his father, a poet and conductor for the village's Dunvant Excelsior Male Voice Choir, might explain why music and verse were often at the heart of his work.

Having moved to London to study at the Royal College of Art, exposure to the likes of Pablo Picasso and Jean Arp drew him into the world of surrealism, and he exhibited in the International Surrealist Exhibition of 1936. A talented pianist as well as an artist, music found expression in his works such as *La Cathédrale Engloutie,* a series based on Debussy's *Preludes*, and his *Beethoven Suite with Variations*, which includes a portrait of the German composer.

He also illustrated the words of his hometown poets Vernon Watkins and Dylan Thomas, notably Thomas' *The force that through the green fuse drives the flower* in a series of lithographs commissioned by Poetry London.

The Ceri Richards Gallery, which has a year-round calendar of exhibitions and displays, was opened in Swansea University's Taliesin Arts Centre in 1984.

Alfred Janes: Swansea-born Alfred Janes (1911–1999), a friend of Ceri Richards who shared his love for art and music, painted several notable portraits of his Kardomah Gang contemporaries including Vernon Watkins and Daniel Jones, which can be found in the collections of the Glyn Vivian Art Gallery and National Museum Wales.

While studying at London's Royal Academy of Arts, he shared accommodation with two other subjects of his portraits, Mervyn Levy and Dylan Thomas, but when he returned to his hometown he abandoned his paintings, many of which were lost forever. Fortunately, fellow artists Cedric Morris and Augustus John were curating a Welsh art exhibition at the time, and were able to salvage some of his work, including one of his three portraits of Thomas.

Along with his portraits, Janes is remembered for his unique still lifes, which were painstakingly detailed and notoriously time-consuming.

Ernest Zobole: The Rhondda Valleys would have a profound effect on oil painter Ernest Zobole (1927–1999), who was born there, died there, and used the area – its streets, its people, its railways and coalfields – as a muse for his dreamlike paintings.

Of Italian heritage, Zobole studied at Cardiff College of Art, and it was while commuting each day with five of his colleagues that the Rhondda Group was born, a forward-looking movement of eager young artists with an international outlook.

After spending time in the army and teaching in Anglesey, Zobole entered his most daring and experimental phase of painting in the 1960s when he embraced expressionism and switched from painting on canvas to painting on board. An early painting from this period, *People and Ystrad Rhondda* (1961), can be seen at National Museum Wales.

Upon retiring from Newport School of Art in 1984, Zobole spent his final years painting in his beloved village of Ystrad.

Evan Walters: With the benefit of hindsight, Evan Walters (1893–1951) could be seen as a visionary painter who was years ahead of his time. Unfortunately, in his own lifetime, he was seen by many as a talented artist who squandered his abilities on inexplicable works of art.

Born in Llangyfelach, Swansea, it was the backing of the philanthropist Winifred Coombe Tennant that allowed Walters the opportunity to develop as a portrait painter, but it also afforded him the freedom to experiment, and he became obsessed with the notion of 'double vision' in a painting, which amounted to blurring objects and backgrounds to give an almost 3D effect to their focal point.

His enthusiasm for his new method was not shared by the public, or by his patron, who insisted that her portrait – which would prove to be Walters' final portrait – was painted 'normally'.

BRITAIN'S RICHEST LIVING PAINTER

He might not be a household name in his homeland, but in 2004 **Andrew Vicari** (b. 20 April 1938) was said to be Britain's richest living painter thanks to the global demand for his oil-based portraits, most notably in the Middle East where there are three museums dedicated solely to his work.

Born to Italian parents who had immigrated to Port Talbot from Parma, Vicari showed promise from an early age by winning the National Eisteddfod's gold medal for painting at the age of 12, an award which he has since credited with giving him the confidence to pursue a career in art.

Having studied at Swansea School of Art, Vicari headed to London's Slade School of Fine Art, the youngest student to be admitted at the

Andrew Vicari at Dylan Thomas' birthplace, 5 Cwmdonkin Drive, Swansea, 2015. (*South Wales Evening Post* / Gayle Marsh)

time, where he was tutored by Lucian Freud, encouraged by Francis Bacon, and befriended by Augustus John who sat for several portraits.

Immersing himself in Arab culture, Vicari become the official painter of Saudi Arabia in 1974 where he created *The Triumph of the Bedouin*, an epic sixty-piece history of the country, and his fame soon spread further afield throughout Asia.

Back home, Vicari created the first piece of art for Cardiff's Millennium Stadium, *The Millennium Stadium Vigonade*, and was called upon by the same venue to act as a painter-cum-exorcist to help cure the supposedly cursed south changing room by painting it with a red mural. No team stationed in the 'room of doom' had won a match before, until a week after Vicari's mural when Stoke emerged as victors of the Division Two play-off final.

MODERN-DAY ART IN WALES

The modern-day art scene in Wales is nothing if not varied, and diverse works of contemporary, conceptual and installation art can be found in most major towns and cities. **CASW** (Contemporary Art Society for Wales), established in 1937 with Augustus John at the helm, aim to foster a greater understanding of the arts, from grassroots education to purchasing artworks for donation.

Marc Rees' Adain Avion, a converted DC-9 in Swansea, 2012.
(*South Wales Evening Post*)

Significant contributors include the politically and culturally motivated **Ivor Davies**, who created art using explosives in the 1960s; Swansea's **Nick Holly**, who has been dubbed 'the Welsh L.S. Lowry', a title shared with the late Jack Jones; the emotionally charged paintings of Australian-born **Shani Rhys James**, which are characterised by their powerful use of colour and abstract elements; the striking pop art of **Ken Elias**, who uses a range of media in his bold creations; Porthmadog's **Rob Piercy**, who combines his passion for mountaineering with landscape painting, particularly in his native Snowdon; and **Clive Hicks-Jenkins**, renowned for his narrative art and described by actor Simon Callow as 'one of the most individual and complete artists of our time'.

Pushing the boundaries with their installation and performance-based works are the likes of **Bedwyr Williams**, who introduces humour and stand-up comedy into his often autobiographical works, and **Marc Rees**, whose immersive, community-based projects include 2012's ambitious Adain Avion, in which the fuselage of a disused plane was converted into a mobile art space and toured across the country.

ARTES MUNDI

Founded by Welsh pointillist artist **William Wilkins** in 2002, the non-profit charity Artes Mundi, whose Latin name translates as arts of the world, hosts a biennial contemporary art exhibition and prize in Cardiff which sees some of the world's leading emerging artists display their works across the capital, traditionally at National Museum Cardiff but also incorporating other local venues.

With a cash prize of £40,000 – which American winner Theaster Gates generously shared with his fellow nominees in 2015 – and over 700 entries from ninety countries for Artes Mundi 7, it has been described as 'the biggest arts prize in the UK'.

Playing an active role in developing links with the local communities and encouraging social engagement with art, the event is accompanied by workshops and resources, with ongoing activities and research that continue after the award itself.

WALES AT THE VENICE BIENNALE

In 2003, Wales introduced its own pavilion to another biennial contemporary art exhibition, the prestigious Venice Biennale in Italy, which sees artists from around the world displaying their work on a global stage.

Previously, Welsh artists, such as Ceri Richards and Barry Flanagan, had been a part of the British Council's British Pavilion, and were exhibited alongside artists from the rest of the UK.

Representing Wales at their initial solo exhibition were Bethan Huws, Cerith Wyn Evans and Simon Pope, who have been followed by the likes of Bedwyr Williams, John Cale, Tim Davies, Heather and Ivan Morison and Helen Sear.

GOLD MEDALS

The National Eisteddfod annually awards three gold medals for art, in the categories of fine art since 1951, craft and design since 1985 and, most recently, for architecture since 2005, with Capita Percy Thomas winning the initial medal for the Wales Millennium Centre.

Seen as a rite of passage for many Welsh artists, fine art winners have included Brenda Chamberlain who claimed the first two medals in 1951 and 1953, Ceri Richards in 1961, Josef Herman in 1962 and Shani Rhys James in 1992.

In 2007, the judges caused something of a stir when they decided not to award a medal in the craft and design category due to what they considered to be a lack of quality in the submissions.

GALLERIES TO VISIT

National Museum of Art, Cardiff: The jewel in the crown of Welsh art galleries, Cardiff's National Museum houses the largest collection of paintings, drawings, sculpture and ceramics in Wales, with works of Welsh and international importance that span over 500 years.

Welsh highlights include the changing Faces from Wales display, an extensive collection of Welsh pottery and porcelain, and iconic works from the likes of landscape masters Richard Wilson and Thomas Jones to twentieth-century visionaries Augustus John and Kyffin Williams.

Its impressive international art collection includes a vast selection of Impressionist paintings, which includes work by Renoir, Monet and van Gogh.

Glynn Vivian Art Gallery, Swansea: The Glynn Vivian, Swansea's leading art gallery, was established in 1911 with the collection of Richard

Glynn Vivian, who donated his diverse range of paintings, drawing and Swansea china to the city in 1905. The permanent collection has been continuously added to, and includes major works from local artists including Ceri Richards, Alfred Janes and Josef Herman.

Martin Tinney Gallery, Cardiff: Martin Tinney's gallery in Cardiff, who also owns Anglesey's Oriel Tegfryn, is a private, commercial gallery that offers a wide range of contemporary art from leading living and emerging artists such as Harry Holland and Shani Rhys James, alongside works from twentieth-century artists and monthly solo exhibitions.

Oriel Mostyn Gallery, Llandudno: Wales's largest publicly funded contemporary art institution, Oriel Mostyn aims to be both educational and inclusive, and utilises its six gallery spaces to display work from Wales and around the world in its changing exhibitions.

Oriel Ynys Môn, Llangefni: Anglesey's centre for art and history has a main gallery for its larger exhibitions, alongside long and central galleries. It houses Oriel Kyffin Williams, which was established by the Kyffin Williams Trust to promote the work of the artist, who also run the triennial Kyffin Williams Drawing Prize for young artists.

Oriel Plas Glyn-y-Weddw, Llanbedrog, Pwllheli: Wales' oldest art gallery, which hosts changing modern art exhibitions, can be found in a stunning grade two Victorian Gothic mansion, originally a dower house built in 1856 for the personal collection of Lady Elizabeth Love Jones-Parry.

Museum of Modern Art, Machynlleth: MOMA's six exhibition spaces house the changing Modern Welsh Art exhibition alongside a permanent collection from artists living or working in Wales from 1900, including John Piper, Peter Blake, Frank Brangwyn, and Mervyn Levy's drawings of his friend Dylan Thomas. Set alongside the performing arts centre Y Tabernacl, its plays an active role in the annual Machynlleth Festival and hosts the Tabernacle Art Competition.

Oriel y Parc Gallery, Saint Davids: Pembrokeshire had a profound effect on English artist Graham Sutherland, who bequeathed a selection of his work to the county, which can often be seen in Oriel y Parc's landscape gallery. It also hosts family and community-based activities, and has an artist-in-residence studio and a tower for local arts.

Oriel Myrddin Gallery, Carmarthen: A vibrant, contemporary gallery based in a former Victorian school building in the heart of Carmarthen, Oriel Myrddin opened in 1991 with a core set of principles established in 1892 by Carmarthen School of Art, which includes free and accessible art for all. It hosts temporary exhibitions with educational programmes.

Oriel Wrecsam: The temporary home of contemporary visual and applied arts in North East Wales can be found on Chester Street in Wrexham's town centre. In 2018, Oriel Wrecsam will relocate to the new £4.3 million Arts and Cultural Space designed by Featherstone Young Architects in The People's Market. Their innovative approach to the arts includes the Art Vend project, in which miniature works of art can be bought by inserting £1 into a vending machine.

COMIC ART

Wales' leading satirist **J.M. Staniforth** (1863–1921), who was born in Gloucester but moved to Cardiff at the age of 7, captured the country's social turmoil up until the First World War with his tongue-in-cheek drawings for the *Western Mail*. His most enduring character, Mam Cymru / Dame Wales, was intended to be the Welsh equivalent of England's John Bull. She is pictured above in *The Royal Visit*, 1899.

Comic strip artist **Grenfell 'Gren' Jones** (1934–2007) from Hengoed, Rhymney Valley, more playfully satirised valley life in his daily cartoon for the *South Wales Echo*. The residents of the fictional village Aberflyarff, who featured in the weekly Ponty an' Pop strip, would go on to find life outside the printed page on radio and TV. Prolific at producing calendars and books, Gren was named UK Provincial

Cartoonist of the Year on four occasions, and his drawing for the cover to Max Boyce's chart-topping album *We All Had Doctors' Papers* made him the first cartoonist to be given a gold disc.

The Welsh have long had an appetite for American comic books, with specialist stockists such as Swansea's Comix Shoppe, which opened in 1986 and is still going strong, and annual conventions – complete with cosplay (costume play) – held in towns and cities including Wrexham, Cardiff and Port Talbot.

Welsh artists and writers who have contributed to the art form stateside include Swansea's **Anthony Williams**, who has drawn the adventures of DC superheroes Batman and Superman, and **Paul Jenkins**, who befriended Teenage Mutant Ninja Turtles creators Kevin Eastman and Peter Laird early in his career while working as an editor for Mirage Studios, and has written the likes of *Hellblazer* for Vertigo and *Spider-Man* for Marvel.

Welsh characters in American funnybooks are few and far between, but include the X-Men's Pixie (Megan Gwynn) and the villainous Damian Tryp (Dafydd ap Andras) from Marvel, as well as two characters both named Captain Cymru, in Marvel Comics as Morwen Powell and – very fleetingly – in DC Comics' Justice League Europe.

Cardiff-based artist and writer **Mike Collins**, who has also worked for the American 'big two', created the first Welsh-language graphic novel in 2003, *Y Mabinogi*, while the first home-grown Welsh-language comic, *Hwyl* (Fun), was launched by Ifor Owens in 1949.

FASHION DESIGNERS

Laura Ashley: Despite living in London at the time, Laura Ashley's (1925–1985) mother returned home to Merthyr Tydfil to ensure that her daughter was born in Wales, and it was there that her grandmother fostered a passion for quilting, a passion which the self-taught fashion and fabric designer would develop into a world-famous business in later life.

Along with husband Sir Bernard Ashley, Ashley initially achieved success with the production of headscarves and tea towels in 1953 from their home in London, which were created using natural fabrics and printed with what would become known as her distinctive style.

The company soon expanded into a family retail and manufacturing business, relocating to Wales in the 1960s where they opened a shop in Machynlleth before settling at the Old Railway House in Carno to mass-produce clothing and items for the home.

Jeff Banks: A contemporary yet affordable approach to design saw Jeff Banks (b. 1943) named as British Designer of the Year in 1979 and 1981, as well as British Coat Designer of the Year in 1980 – not bad for a boy from Ebbw Vale whose father had to mortgage his house to help him open his first London boutique in 1964.

The success of Clobber, which sold Banks' designs alongside those of other designers, would allow him to launch his own fashion label five years later, and it wasn't long before he had his own Jeff Banks store and outlets in such prestigious locations as Harrods.

Banks' growing reputation allowed him to branch out into a career in the media, notably as the presenter for the BBC's leading fashion show *The Clothes Show* from its launch in 1986.

David Emanuel: Flamboyant fashion designer David Emanuel (b. 1952) is probably most famous for designing the wedding dress for Diana, Princess of Wales, in 1981, as well as being a familiar face on television as a presenter, a guest expert, and as a contestant on TV shows such as *I'm a Celebrity … Get Me Out of Here!*

Born in Bridgend, Emanuel's first love was music, as a choirboy, violinist and cellist, but he declined the offer to attend the Welsh College of Music and Drama to follow a career in design, meeting his now ex-wife and fellow designer Elizabeth while studying Fashion Design at Harrow School of Art.

Outside of fashion, Emanuel's career has included designing sets and wardrobes for stage and screen, while his client list of the rich and famous includes Welsh celebrities Shirley Bassey and Catherine Zeta-Jones.

Julien Macdonald: Having been taught to knit by his mother while growing up in Merthyr Tydfil, Julien Macdonald (b. 1972) would go on to design for the likes of Kylie Minogue and Naomi Campbell, and has a CV that can boast being chief designer for Givenchy, launching his own company, and claiming the title of British Designer of the Year in 2001.

Torn between pursuing a career in dance or fashion, Macdonald opted to study textiles at Brighton, and it wasn't long after graduating from the Royal College of Art that he picked up his first job with Chanel.

A regular face on television, Macdonald has been a judge on *Project Catwalk* and *Britain's Next Top Model*, and a contestant on *Strictly Come Dancing*.

JEWELLERY

Welsh jewellers of note include Clogau Gold, whose incredible origin lies in an abandoned goldmine discovered in Snowdonia by William Roberts in 1989. The initial idea was to convert it into a tourist attraction, but having been denied permission, Roberts instead – quite literally – struck gold while exploring the mine, which has been used to create distinctly Welsh jewellery which is sold the world over, and used for wedding rings by Hollywood stars and royalty.

Mari Thomas Jewellery, based in Llandeilo, is led by the award-winning contemporary designer who has not only won awards at the National Eisteddfod, but has designed the crowns for the festival as well, and can count the likes of Catherine Zeta-Jones and the Welsh Rugby Union among her clients.

6

WALES ON STAGE

The origins of theatre in Wales are closely linked with the Christian religion, which played an important part in developing – and later suppressing – homegrown drama.

It formed the basis of the first known plays to be written in the country, but subdued its flourishing when faced with works that it deemed inappropriate, and while the remains of an amphitheatre in Caerleon suggest that drama in some shape or form could have been performed on Welsh soil during the Roman occupation, the earliest known works to be written in Welsh are two medieval mystery plays dating from the fifteenth century: *Y Tri Brenin o Gwlen* (The Three Kings from Cologne), a morality play about the Nativity, and *Y Dioddefaint a'r Atgyfodiad* (The Passion and Resurrection), the story of Christ's crucifixion.

During the sixteenth and seventeenth centuries, wealthy patronages and areas large enough to sustain a stage saw theatre flourish across the border in England, but Wales had to content itself predominantly with visiting troupes.

In fact, it is the English dramatists of the period, who used Welsh words, people and places in their plays, that we have to thank for maintaining a continued Welsh presence in the drama of the time, with the highest profile of these written by the world's greatest playwright himself.

William Shakespeare, who was part-Welsh due to his maternal grandmother Alys Griffin, included several Welsh characters in his work, most notably the comical parson Sir Hugh Evans in *The Merry Wives of Windsor*, Captain Fluellen in *Henry V*, and the leader of the Welsh rebels, Owen Glendower (Owain Glyndŵr), in *Henry IV, Part I*. The tragic romance *Cymbeline* is set predominantly in Wales, in which Imogen, the daughter of the King of Britain, makes her way to Milford Haven through the treacherous Welsh mountains.

THE CAMBRIAN SHAKESPEARE

Twm o'r Nant, the people's – if not the establishment's – champion, was labelled The Cambrian Shakespeare by David Samwell, Captain Cook's Welsh naval surgeon, after he failed to win at the Gwyneddigion Society's Corwen eisteddfod in 1789.

It was the one and only time that the dramatist and poet entered the competition, and it is thought that he lost out unfairly to Gwallter Mechain, who was seen as a more respectable winner, and was instead awarded a silver pen, a token gesture which is now a part of the collection of National Museum Wales.

Engraving of Twm o'r Nant from *Ceinion Llenyddiaeth Gymreig*, 1876.

Born Thomas Edwards (1739–1810) in Llannefydd, Denbighshire, it was under his pseudonym, which translates as Twm of the Stream and derives from his parents' home in Y Nant Isaf, that he became known for his anterliwtau (interludes), which were performed on makeshift stages outdoors.

Despite his father's disapproval of his chosen profession, and with only two weeks of formal education, Edwards was determined to write, and even resorted to using elderberry juice as ink when needed. By the age of 9 he'd penned hundreds of plays, and by the age of 12 he was touring Denbighshire with a company of local actors.

His interludes were often a satirical commentary on topical social themes, with the Church being a favoured target for his barbed words, but fame also brought notoriety, and close scrutiny from the men of the cloth.

Edwards would travel across Wales, sometimes for work, sometimes on the run from the bailiffs, but it wasn't until the commercial success of his first book of poems that he was able to clear his debts and return home to Denbighshire, where he continued to write until the end of his life – even carving his own epitaph on his tombstone.

A memorial to Edwards can be found at St Marcella's church in Denbigh.

THE GOLDEN AGE OF THEATRE

Religious opposition to drama continued up until the twentieth century, with the Methodist Convention in 1887 going so far as to suggest that theatre should be classed in the same morally bankrupt category as gambling.

But it received a boost in respectability and a powerful backer in 1902 when David Lloyd George led a call for it to be represented at the National Eisteddfod, and the amateur dramatics scene, a strong social gathering which united communities much like the male voice choirs had done previously, flourished during what has been described as the golden age of am dram.

Founded in 1924, **Swansea Little Theatre,** of which Dylan Thomas was briefly a member and who gave Anthony Hopkins his first break on stage, are thought to be Wales' longest-running amateur group. In 1939, they stuck to the old adage of 'the show must go on' when a wireless was brought onstage to inform the audience that a state of war now existed between Britain and Germany – only for the play to resume moments later.

Swansea Little Theatre's production of *Under Milk Wood* in the
Dylan Thomas Theatre, 2010. (*South Wales Evening Post*)

Annual pantomimes thrived, a festive family tradition which continues
strong to this day, with the pantomime horse, a staple of early
productions, believed to have Welsh origins due to the *Mabinogion*'s
Rhiannon's connections with the Gaulish horse goddess Epona.

Throughout the twentieth century, social issues became prominent
subjects for Welsh-language playwrights such as **D.T. Davies,
R.G. Berry, John Gwilym Jones, James Kitchener Davies** and **Gwenlyn
Parry**. In the English language, **J.O. Francis** emerged as a leading voice
with 1913's *Change*, set during the riots of the Llanelli railwaymen's
strike, and his most popular work, *The Poacher* (1914). 1954 saw the
New York premiere of the most well-known play to be written by a
Welshman, **Dylan Thomas'** radio 'play for voices' *Under Milk Wood*,
which would prove to be equally popular onstage.

It was during this period that dramatist **Emlyn Williams** (1905–
1987) from Mostyn, Flintshire, became an overnight sensation with
the premier of his physiological thriller *Night Must Fall* (1935), which
has twice been adapted for the big screen. A prominent actor who took
to writing following a nervous breakdown, his next big success came
in 1938 with the semi-autobiographical *The Corn is Green*, influenced
by his time growing up on the Welsh border. The play was also adapted
twice, with Bette Davis starring in the first, followed by a made-for-TV
film shot partly on location in Wales featuring Katharine Hepburn.

Williams gave a young Richard Burton his first break on stage in *The Druid's Rest* (1944), and later on screen in his *The Last Days of Dolwyn* (1949), and worked with Alfred Hitchcock, appearing in *Jamaica Inn* (1939) and writing additional dialogue for *The Man Who Knew Too Much* (1956).

THE NATIONALIST VOICE OF WELSH DRAMA

Saunders Lewis (15 October 1893 – 1 September 1985) was many things – a poet, novelist, historian, critic, fierce nationalist and activist, and founding member of Plaid Genedlaethol Cymru, the National Party of Wales – and as such, his contribution to Welsh drama, which led to him being labelled the country's greatest dramatist, is often overshadowed by his outspoken opinions and controversial actions.

Nominated for the Nobel Prize for Literature in 1970, Saunders published nineteen plays between 1921 and 1980, including his English-language debut *The Eve of St John* (1921), the radio play *Buchedd Garmon* (The Life of Garmon, 1937), which he was allowed to listen to while serving time in prison for the 'Fire in Llŷn' protest, the *Mabinogion*-inspired *Blodeuwedd* (1948), and his most popular works *Siwan* (1956), *Gymerwch chi Sigarét?* (Will you take a cigarette? 1956), *Brad* (Treason, 1958) and *Esther* (1960).

Born John Saunders Lewis in Wallasey, Merseyside, to a Welsh-speaking family, Saunders served with the South Wales Borderers during the First World War, but it was after taking up a lecturing post at Swansea University that he began to develop his nationalistic ideas. At the 1925 National Eisteddfod, Plaid Genedlaethol Cymru were formed following a meeting between Saunders' Mudiad Cymreig (The Welsh Movement) organisation and the Byddin Ymreolwyr Cymru (The Welsh Home Rule Army).

Saunders had a vision of a Wales that was entirely Welsh speaking, and the BBC, which broadcast almost exclusively in English, became a target for his ire. In 1929, he was invited to record a talk on Welsh nationalism, but his call to arms was considered too provocative to be aired.

Undeterred, Saunders would keep up the pressure, joining a committee formed by the university – who would dismiss him following his involvement as one of the Penyberth three – which resulted in the formation of the BBC's Welsh Advisory Council in 1946. Another BBC lecture, 1962's *Tynged yr Iaith* (The Fate of the Language), in which he prophesised the death of the Welsh language unless major action was taken, was pivotal in the formation of Cymdeithas yr Iaith Gymraeg (The Welsh Language Society).

THE ARCHDRUID CENSOR

Poet and dramatist Sir (Albert) Cynan Evans-Jones (14 April 1895 – 26 January 1970) – known by his bardic name Cynan – became inseparable from the National Eisteddfod, and was the only person to be named Archdruid on two separate occasions, to win the chair for a poem that did not conform to the strict rules of cynghanedd, and to be awarded the crown three times for his poems Mab y Bwthyn (A Cottage Son), Yr Ynys Unig (The Lonely Isle), and the first Welsh poem to focus on the game of rugby, Y Dyrfa (The Crowd).

Hailing from Pwllheli, Llŷn Peninsula, Cynan's first full-length play, *Hywel Harris*, won the 1931 prize for drama, while his second, *Absolom Fy Mab* (Absolom My Son), was commissioned by the National Eisteddfod in 1957.

But his impact on Welsh drama extended beyond writing when he was appointed by Lord Chamberlain to act as the Welsh censor for drama, a role which involved reading and approving Welsh-language plays until the need was abolished in 1968.

Cynan was also instrumental in removing any opposition that the Church might have had towards the National Eisteddfod when, during his time as Archdruid, he acknowledged that, in its current incarnation, the festival had no real lineage with ancient Druidic traditions.

A NATIONAL THEATRE FOR WALES

The establishment of a national theatre for Wales was a long drawn-out process, and one which seemed, at times, destined to be little more than a dream.

In a letter to the *South Wales Daily Post* published in 1914, Irish playwright George Bernard Shaw outlined the benefits of such an institution, asking 'if Manchester, Dublin and Glasgow produced, as they did, a genuine indigenous drama almost instantly upon the establishment of a permanent local theatre, what might Wales not do, with its natural wealth of artistic faculty and its sense of nationality?'

Soon after, it was an Englishman with a passion for the culture of his adopted country, London-born peer and author **Thomas Scott-Ellis, 8th Baron Howard de Walden** (1880–1946) who produced theatrical productions under the name T.E. Ellis, who attempted to do just that.

Introduced to North Wales by composer Joseph Holbrooke, he took out a lease on Chirk Castle, Denbighshire, which served as his base from where he could learn the Welsh language, and use his position to promote Welsh talent and extoll the virtues of the eisteddfod.

He would collaborate with Holbrooke on many occasions, notably between 1908 and 1920 when he wrote the libretto for a trilogy of operas based on the *Mabinogion*, beginning with *The Children of Don*, ending with *Bronwen*, and *Dylan: Son of Wave* which premiered in 1914, and is believed to have inspired Dylan Thomas' father when naming his son who was born the same year.

De Walden made two attempts to establish a national theatre in Wales, but both were hampered by war. The first was a Cardiff-based touring company which was aborted after a single season following the outbreak of the First World War, and again in 1933 with the bilingual Welsh National Playhouse based at Plas Newydd, Llangollen, which struggled financially and was closed on the eve of the Second World War in 1939.

Following de Walden, later attempts included the formation of **The Welsh Theatre Company** in 1962, which split into the English-language **Welsh Drama Company** and the Welsh-language **Theatr Cymru** in the early 1970s, while several leading Welsh playwrights led by **Dedwydd Jones** ran a sustained campaign for a national company to promote and develop indigenous talent.

But it wasn't until the start of the twenty-first century that Welsh and English-language national theatre companies finally emerged as distinct entities.

THEATR GENEDLAETHOL CYMRU

Theatr Genedlaethol Cymru, the Welsh-language national theatre, finally saw the light of day in 2003, six years before its English language counterpart.

Based in Carmarthen, the company – the smallest of all British national theatre companies – combines a global outlook with an ethos firmly rooted in local communities. This is reflected in some of its more inventive productions set in unconventional locations, such as 2013's revival of Saunders Lewis' *Blodeuwedd*, and a promenade production of *Blodyn*, a modern-day spin on the tale with song, dance and art performed on the streets of Blaenau Ffestiniog and Talysarn.

Outside of Wales, TGC have performed at major events and festivals including the World Shakespeare Festival and Edinburgh Festival.

NATIONAL THEATRE OF WALES

Launched online in 2009, the English-language National Theatre of Wales began life when a group of likeminded professionals founded an Internet community with the aim of being 'innovative, engaged and international'.

The following year, the company, which has no single base of operations, set out to create a minimum of twelve new productions a year, starting with a performance of Alan Harris' *A Good Night Out in the Valleys* at Blackwood Miners' Institute. The inaugural production, featuring actors and bands from the local area with a raffle and bingo during the show, was a prime example of the company's inclusive, community approach to theatre.

2011 would see NTW make the front pages of the national newspapers when Michael Sheen returned to his hometown to star in *The Passion*, a hugely ambitious, weekend-long public performance during which a bloodied Sheen dragged a crucifix through the streets of Port Talbot in a retelling of the Eastertime Passion play. Written by Owen Sheers, it drew stark parallels to the town's modern-day circumstances, and was later released as the film *The Gospel of Us* (2012).

Continuing to revolutionise with each subsequent release, productions of note include the open-air wartime promenade epic *Mametz* (2014), the marathon, all-day and all-night performances of *Iliad* (2015), and *The Radicalisation of Bradley Manning* (2012), Tim Price's fictionalised life story of the American soldier accused of releasing military information to WikiLeaks, which became the first winner of the University of Edinburgh's James Tait Black Prize for Drama.

Michael Sheen in National Theatre Wales' *The Passion* in Port
Talbot, 2011. (Geraint Lewis / National Theatre Wales)

MODERN-DAY THEATRE

With over 200 production companies in Wales, there is no shortage of diverse styles on offer, with support coming from the likes of **Creu Cymru**, a collaborative network who aim to develop theatrical programmes by sharing knowledge and expertise.

Notable theatres who produce in-house include **Sherman Cymru**'s range of high-quality drama for all ages, Mold's impressive **Theatr Clwyd**, who regularly tour Wales with large-scale productions, many of which are of Welsh origin, and the long-running **Torch Theatre**, Pembrokeshire's only professional theatre company.

The inspirational **Hijinx Theatre** regularly tour with their 'inclusive theatre' productions, which give leading roles to actors with learning disabilities, while **Theatr Bara Caws** provide a wide range of productions from cutting-edge to family friendly, and **Mappa Mundi Theatre Company** put their own original spin on familiar classics.

Volcano Theatre Company, founded in the 1980s by artistic director Paul Davies and Fern Smith, continue to push the boundaries of performance art with an innovate brand of theatre fused with a punk rock ethic, while Cardiff-based fringe company **Dirty Protest** stage exciting and alternative new plays from Welsh writers.

Youth theatre plays an important role in developing talent, with the **National Youth Theatre of Wales**, **West Glamorgan Youth Theatre** and **Theatr Clwyd's Theatre for Young People** among those leading the way.

Playwrights of note include Cardiff's **Peter Gill** (b. 1939), whose career began as an actor in the 1950s, but excelled as a writer and director, most notably in his role as Associate Director at England's National Theatre from 1980 until succeeded by Sir Richard Eyre in 1997. His plays include *The Sleepers Den* (1965), *The York Realist* (2002) and *Versailles* (2014).

The plays of Treorchy's **Frank Vickery** remain perennial favourites, which aim to be both funny and poignant and are populated with characters firmly rooted in his native South Wales, while key contemporary playwrights include Cardiff-born **Dic Edwards**, Tredegar's **Patrick Jones**, and Haverfordwest's **Gary Owen**.

SHAKING UP THE ESTABLISHMENT

It was while working as associate director for the Royal National Theatre in 1980 that Neath-born director Michael Bogdanov (b. 15 December 1938) suffered the wrath of notorious moral protector Mary Whitehouse, who labelled a simulated anal rape scene in his production of Howard Brenton's *The Romans in Britain* as an act of 'gross indecency'.

The case went to London's Old Bailey, but was unexpectedly dropped at the eleventh hour by Whitehouse's barrister.

Following the controversy, Bogdanov founded the English Shakespeare Company in 1986 with Michael Pennington, and would win the Laurence Olivier Award for Best Director in 1990 for the seven consecutive plays which formed the epic *The Wars of the Roses* history cycle.

Despite being in demand across the world, Bogdanov regularly finds time to return home to Wales to direct at Swansea Grand Theatre, to mentor students at Gorseinon College, and helped found the Wales Theatre Company in 2003.

His notable productions on Welsh soil include Mal Pope's musical *Amazing Grace*, *Hamlet* performed in both English and Welsh by the same cast, and the mammoth 36-hour *Dylathon*, which saw the likes of Sir Ian McKellen and Irish president Michael Daniel Higgins take to the stage of Swansea Grand Theatre to mark Dylan Thomas' centenary in 2014.

MUSICAL THEATRE

Of all the Welsh performers to star in musicals, it was Port Talbot's **Ivor Emmanuel** (1927–2007) who personified everything that it was to be a Welshman in the 1960s following his iconic portrayal of Private Owen in the war film *Zulu* (1964), who rallied the troops in a rousing chorus of 'Men of Harlech'.

Making his stage debut in *Oklahoma!* after receiving a telegram from Pontrhydyfen drinking buddy Richard Burton who told him to be at Drury Lane's Theatre Royal for an audition the next day, it wasn't long before he'd established himself in the West End and made his Broadway debut in *How Green Was My Valley, A Time for Singing*. On television, Emmanuel sang on Welsh TV shows *Dewch i Mewn* (Come on in) and *Gwlad y Gân* (Land of Song) which, at the time, were broadcast across the UK, exposing Emmanuel – and the language – to a wider audience.

Broadway to the Bay, created by Wales Millennium Centre with
David Mahoney and John Owen-Jones. (Polly Thomas)

In later years, Andrew Lloyd Webber's conveyor belt of hits proved to
be highly successful for the likes of **Shân Cothi**, **Ria Jones** and **Mike
Sterling**, with Swansea's **Steve Balsamo** taking the title role in 1996's
award-winning revival of *Jesus Christ Superstar*, and Burry Port's **John
Owen-Jones** becoming the youngest person to tackle Jean Valjean in a
full-time production of *Les Misérables* at the age of 26.

Michael Ball, born in Worcestershire to Welsh parents, established a
musical theatre career which crossed over into television and the charts,
taking the role of Marius Pontmercy in the original 1985 London cast
for *Les Misérables*, and later reaching number two with the single
'Love Changes Everything' from 1989's *Aspects of Love*.

Aled Jones also carved out a similar crossover career in music,
broadcasting and stage, but will, invariably, always be synonymous
with his initial breakthrough hit, Howard Blake's theme tune to
Raymond Briggs' animated adventure *The Snowman* (1982), 'Walking
in the Air'. Re-recorded by the boy soprano from Bangor for a Toys
R Us TV commercial in 1985, Jones went on an impressive run of
selling millions of albums before making his stage debut in Welsh
favourite *How Green Was My Valley* in 1990, later making his musical
debut in *Joseph and the Amazing Technicolour Dreamcoat* in 1995.

Off the stage, Llanelli-born lyricist **Julian More** was responsible for
three of the biggest musicals of the 1950s, the comedies *Grab Me a
Gondola*, *Expresso Bongo* and *Irma La Douce*, while the works of
Roald Dahl continue to make the leap from page to stage in West End
hits such as *Matilda* and *Charlie and the Chocolate Factory*.

In 1971, *Tom Jones Slept Here* by **John Lewis Hughes** became the country's first rock musical, while **Theatr na nÓg** took their musical *Tom*, based on the life and music of the singer, on a national tour in 2016.

IVOR NOVELLO

A star in every sense of the word, composer and actor Ivor Novello – Cardiff's David Ivor Davies (15 January 1893 – 6 March 1951) – dominated the world of entertainment in the first half of the twentieth century.

Musically, the First World War was a fruitful period for Novello, with his *Keep the Home Fires Burning* emerging as a wartime anthem, and comedy *Theodore & Co.* (1917) becoming his first big musical theatre hit. But he was less successful as a soldier, twice crashing an aeroplane at the Royal Naval Air Service training ground and given clerical duties to attend to instead.

Following the conflict, he turned his attentions to acting, with his role as a dark and mysterious stranger in Alfred Hitchcock's *The Lodger* (1927) said to have been the inspiration for Norman Bates in the director's future horror hit *Psycho*. As a writer, he is credited with coining the phrase 'Me Tarzan, you Jane' in *Tarzan the Ape Man* (1932).

Back in the West End, Novello ruled the stage in the 1930s and '40s, composing a string of hit shows which started with 1935's *Glamorous Night* through to his final offering, 1951's *Gay's the Word*.

A statue of Novello now sits proudly outside the Wales Millennium Centre in Cardiff Bay.

THE CAPPUCCINO BOY

Possibly the most accomplished Welsh musicals to be written in the twenty-first century have come from the pen of Swansea's jack-of-all-trades **Mal Pope** (b. 1960), who started his career as a singer-songwriter by signing for Elton John's The Rocket Record Company, and wrote songs for the likes of Cliff Richard and The Hollies.

A familiar face and voice on Welsh television and radio, Pope's first musical, *Amazing Grace* (2005), based on the Welsh Christian revival at the turn of the twentieth century, premiered at Swansea Grand Theatre and became the first Welsh musical to be performed at Wales Millennium Centre. His 2007 follow-up *The Contender*, the story of Welsh boxer Tommy Farr – the Tonypandy Terror – who controversially lost to American champion Joe Louis, premiered at New York's United Nations Headquarters.

The 'unique theatrical dining experience' *Cappuccino Girls* originally opened in 2009, but it wasn't until 2015 that Pope was able to realise his original vision of staging the musical, a heartfelt tale of three women who solve life's problems over a cup of coffee, in a café setting, with Swansea's Coast Italia allowing the audience to dine while the actors perform around them.

LET'S DANCE

Dancing in Wales can be traced back to the twelfth century when it was centred around the annual festivals. Its fortunes mirrored those of the country's folk music, which flourished until the Industrial Revolution brought new, imported distractions to the land, and coupled with a stern Nonconformist disapproval saw a rapid decline which all but wiped out the tradition.

Despite this, clog dancing, which is driven by the sounds of hard wooden shoes hitting the floor, has remained relatively unchanged throughout history, and its inclusion in eisteddfodau has given it a competitive edge.

Folk dancing is also represented at eisteddfods, and the formation of the **Welsh Folk Dance Society** in 1949 played an important part in reviving the tradition. It found further impetus a decade later with the introduction of Urdd Gobaith Cymru's twmpath dawns (barn dance), a relaxed, fun approach to dancing which proved popular with the young. The twmpath is still included in Welsh language school events and gatherings today, along with Noson Lawen, a party with music.

National Dance Company Wales, formed in 1983 as Diversions by Roy Campbell-Moore and Ann Sholem, is the country's leading producer of contemporary dance. Based in the Dance House at Cardiff's Wales Millennium Centre, it performs the works of acclaimed international choreographers, and actively engages in educating and nurturing the next generation of Welsh dancers with an extensive range of classes and courses.

While Wales has no classical ballet heritage to speak of, the eight-strong team of dancers that form **Ballet Cymru** have given the country a ballet company to be proud of. Established in 1986 by Darius

James and Yvonne Williams, the Newport-based team tour the UK with their experimental performances, which give new slants to Shakespearian and fairy tale favourites, as well as those that reference their Welsh heritage.

AWARDS

Wales Theatre Awards: Held annually at Cardiff's Sherman Cymru, the independent Wales Theatre Awards celebrate the best in home-grown Welsh and English-language theatre, opera and dance.

Having begun life in 2013 as the Theatre Critics of Wales Awards, which emerged from the Young Critics Wales scheme that helps to develop the skills of young reviewers, the awards were expanded and rebranded in 2014 under director Mike Smith.

Quickly establishing itself as a crucial and much-needed event in the Welsh cultural calendar, the awards are run in association with the Critics Fund, which aims to broaden the spectrum of criticism in Wales with financial assistance and expertise.

The Wales Drama Award: The biennial Wales Drama Award, which offers a prize of £10,000 and an opportunity for the winning script to be developed by a national theatre company and broadcaster, is the largest competition available for Welsh drama writers. Launched in

The winners of the Wales Theatre Awards 2015. (Natasha Hirst Photography)

2012 by National Theatre Wales, in partnership with BBC Cymru Wales TV Drama, entries can be submitted in any medium, with a winner selected from a shortlist of four finalists.

A NEW CENTRE FOR A NEW MILLENNIUM

The Wales Millennium Centre, opened by Her Majesty the Queen to much fanfare on 28 November 2004, is Wales' leading establishment for the arts, welcoming some of the largest touring productions to Wales while supporting some of the best new works of Welsh origin and collaborating with leading companies across the world.

Designed by Jonathan Adams of Percy Thomas Architects, the Centre's distinctive bronze dome, inscribed with the poetry of Gwyneth Lewis above layers of Welsh slate, has made Wales' national arts centre Cardiff Bay's most iconic landmark, and is home to several national companies including Welsh National Opera, BBC National Orchestra of Wales and Literature Wales.

Established following the aborted attempt to create a Cardiff Bay Opera House, large-scale musical and operatic productions are performed in the Donald Gordon Theatre, a lyric theatre with

Wales Millennium Centre. (Phil Boorman)

a capacity of 1,900, along with performances in the Weston Studio Theatre, the Dance Hall and BBC Hoddinott Hall for orchestral music.

With a large programme of events, it engages with young people through its Creative Learning and Community Engagement programmes, and its range of shops, bars, cafes and art exhibitions, along with free performances in the foyer, make it a popular tourist destination for those with and without tickets.

Cultural highlights to date include the inaugural Cymru for the World ceremony which honoured Shirley Bassey, Gwyneth Jones, Siân Phillips, Alun Hoddinott and Richard Burton during its opening weekend, the UK premiere of Mariinsky Opera's Wagner's *Ring Cycle* (tickets for which sold out in under four hours), and a series of major ten-year anniversary celebrations in 2015, which saw the Centre's ambassador Bryn Terfel join the WNO for two concert performances, and the epic *Ar Waith Ar Daith*, a free, outdoor, bilingual celebration of Welsh culture featuring more than 600 performers led by Shân Cothi as Ceridwen, the enchantress from Welsh legend. In 2016, Wales Millennium Centre staged their first home-produced musical, *Only the Brave*.

TEN THEATRES TO VISIT

Most areas of Wales are within a short driving distance of a stage, from bustling arts centres such as Pontypridd's **The Muni Arts Centre** and Swansea's **Taliesin Arts Centre** to seaside venues like Porthcawl's **Grand Pavilion** and **Aberystwyth's Art Centre** and the valley strongholds of Aberdare's **The Coliseum** and Treorchy's **Park and Dare**. In 2016, Bangor University unveiled their state-of-the-art **Pontio** arts and innovation centre for performing arts.

Below is a selection of ten venues that either have historical significance, or are important backers of home-grown productions.

Swansea Grand Theatre: A favourite for local and touring artists alike, Swansea Grand Theatre is a traditional, Victorian theatre that exudes charm and history.

Officially opened in 1897 by opera singer Adelina Patti, whose plaque adorns the main auditorium, it has been home to Swansea's flagship pantomime for over a century, with record-breaking local personality Kevin Johns returning every year since 1999.

The theatre's Arts Wing was added in 1999, with three floors of alternating artwork and displays and its own small-scale performance

Swansea Grand Theatre. (*South Wales Evening Post*)

area. Its resident companies include the Sir Harry Secombe Trust Youth Theatre and Fluellen Theatre Company who, under the helm of artistic director Peter Richards, stage a wide range of works from classics to premieres from Welsh playwrights.

Chapter Arts Centre, Cardiff: Notable for the vibrant social scene which surrounds its café and bar areas, Chapter is a model arts centre which houses two small-scale theatres offering innovative new Welsh productions alongside art galleries, film theatres and over sixty work spaces.

Theatr Clwyd, Mold: The home of one of the country's leading drama production companies, Theatr Clwyd – previously known as Clwyd Theatr Cymru until 2015 – is a major exponent of Welsh touring theatre based in Mold's County Civic Centre. First opened in 1976, it has five auditoriums as well as art galleries and a Theatre for Young People.

New Theatre, Cardiff: A venue with a long history, Cardiff's New Theatre has welcomed the likes of Anna Pavlova and Laurel and Hardy to the capital since opening its doors in 1906. A theatre of firsts, the Grade II listed building staged the Welsh premiere of Dylan Thomas' *Under Milk Wood* in 1956, and the world premiere of Harold Pinter's *The Homecoming* in 1965.

A bust of Gwyn Thomas was unveiled in the foyer in 1993 by Anthony Hopkins, who portrayed the writer in the television film *Selected Exits* in the same year.

Pavilion Theatre, Rhyl: Rhyl has housed a Pavilion theatre since 1891, although its look and location have changed dramatically throughout the years. The grandest of these, with a capacity of 3,000, would have been the initial theatre on Rhyl Pier which was destroyed by a fire in 1901.

The second Pavilion, which has now been demolished, was a highly decorative building and a local landmark which served the community between 1908 and 1974, while the current manifestation, perched on the seafront since 1991, continues the tradition of hosting some of the larger touring productions alongside community-based theatre.

Savoy Theatre, Monmouth: The Grade II listed theatre proudly displays a blue plaque that informs us that it 'occupies what has been called the oldest theatre site in Wales'. Beginning life as the Assembly Rooms, the venue has seen countless name changes and is currently under the care of the Monmouth Savoy Trust, who receive no public funding and is run entirely by volunteers for the benefit of the community.

Sherman Cymru, Cardiff: A leading producer of Welsh theatre, the prolific Sherman Cymru started life in 1973 as the Sherman Theatre, renaming in 2007 after merging with Cardiff-based theatre company Sgript Cymru, who focus on new English- and Welsh-language works by Welsh writers.

Set in the heart of Cardiff city centre, it houses a twin auditorium and offers a community-focused bilingual programme, from children's workshops to opportunities for emerging artists.

Working closely with associate artists and hosting a company in residence, its productions include Gary Owen's acclaimed UK Theatre Award-winning *Iphigenia in Splott* (2015) starring Sophie Melville, which became the first play from a Welsh company to be staged at London's National Theatre.

The Riverfront, Newport: When Newport became a city in 2002, plans were soon being drawn up for a new home of the arts to match its new status. Two years later, Austin-Smith Lord's modern design was unveiled on the bank of the River Usk, with mezzo-soprano Katherine Jenkins performing at the opening concert. The main auditorium is accompanied by The Studio for smaller productions, dance and recording studios, and an art gallery space.

Venue Cymru, Llandudno: Located in a modern-day conference centre on Llandudno's promenade, Venue Cymru stands on the site of the old Victoria Palace theatre, which opened in 1894.

The theatre has gone through several incarnations, most notably as the Arcadia in 1916 after being bought by Will Catlin, during which period it became the home of the famous Pierrot clowns troupe Catlin's Follies. The derelict Arcadia was pulled down in 2005 to make way for a new development where Venue Cymru now stands, which was named following a competition in a local newspaper.

FILM, TV AND RADIO

THE BIRTH OF BROADCASTING

Broadcasting in Wales was born at 5 p.m. on 13 February 1923, when the first broadcast was beamed from 5WA above a music shop in Cardiff's Castle Street.

Four and a half hours later, David Owen's 'Dafydd y Garreg Wen' (David of the White Rock) became the first Welsh-language song to be sung on air by baritone Mostyn Thomas, and the fledgling radio station soon became a part of the British Broadcasting Corporation's BBC Regional Programme.

A new studio opened in Bangor in 1935 and a dedicated Welsh service was launched in 1937 following a heated struggle led by Saunders Lewis. The outbreak of the Second World War saw all regional radio suspended, and as a result, material which had previously been exclusive to Welsh ears was transmitted to the whole of the UK, bringing the 1940 National Eisteddfod and the English-language comedy Welsh Rarebit to a much wider audience. It also allowed Welsh language listeners to catch the latest news an hour early, which was broadcast in Welsh ahead of the news in English.

TELEVISION

With the opening of a transmitter in Wenvoe, television signals began on 15 August 1952, and a religious service from Cardiff on St David's Day 1953 became the first Welsh-language programme broadcast on television.

In 1957, content aimed purely at a Welsh audience was commissioned by the Bristol-based BBC West region, beginning with a short daily news bulletin presented by Michael Aspel which grew into the long-running national news programme *BBC Wales Today*.

The 1950s also saw the emergence of commercial television channels – commercial radio stations followed in 1974 with the launch of Swansea Sound – with TWW (Television West and Wales) available to many in the south, and Manchester's Granada in the north east, which actually provided more Welsh-language output than the BBC.

In 1964, Wales received its own dedicated national broadcaster: BBC Cymru Wales.

BBC CYMRU WALES

BBC Cymru Wales is the national broadcaster for Wales and produces English and Welsh-language content for television, radio and the Internet.

Its two television channels, BBC One Wales and BBC Two Wales, broadcast a mixture of original Welsh content and programmes from their national counterparts, while its two radio stations, the Welsh-language BBC Radio Cymru and the English-language BBC Radio Wales, provide national news, sport and lifestyle coverage, with a regular *Arts Show* presented by Nicola Heywood Thomas.

In the twenty-first century, investment in new studios has seen a huge increase in the quality of programmes made in Wales, with its drama output, spearheaded by *Doctor Who* and bolstered by commissions like *Sherlock* and *Merlin*, gaining a worldwide following. It has also seen national shows such as *Casualty* and *Upstairs Downstairs* relocate to Cardiff's Roath Studios.

Home-grown productions of note include the drama series *Belonging*, which followed the lives of the Lewis family from Bryncoed from 1999 to 2009, and two of the more memorable sitcoms to emerge from Wales, *Satellite City*, which began on radio in 1994 and later on television between 1996 and 1999, and *High Hopes*, which launched with a pilot in 1999. Both co-written by actor Boyd Clack, *High Hopes* was produced and directed by *Only Fools and Horses* director and later BBC Wales' Head of Comedy Gareth Gwenlan, and starred Robert Blythe and Margaret John as the mother and son of the dysfunctional Hepplewhite family.

ITV CYMRU WALES

ITV Cymru Wales is Wales' dedicated commercial channel, and provides a mixture of national and localised content.

Having started life as HTV (Harlech Television, named after the head of the company, Lord Harlech), it launched on 20 May 1968 with a variety special, and quickly bolstered its board of directors by signing up some of the period's biggest Welsh names, including Richard Burton and his wife Elizabeth Taylor, veteran broadcaster Wynford Vaughan-Thomas and Sir Harry Secombe.

The channel has produced some of the Welsh language's more endearing shows, including S4C favourites *Cefn Gwlad* and *Sion a Siân,* and children's hits *Miri Mawr* and *Ffalabalam.*

S4C

S4C (Sianel Pedwar Cymru/ Channel Four Wales) is Wales' only dedicated Welsh-language television channel, offering programmes which can be watched with English subtitles, and some with simplified Welsh subtitles for those learning the language.

Launched in 1982, a day before the UK-wide Channel 4, it is the fifth oldest channel in the UK, and has been broadcasting entirely in Welsh since the introduction of digital television.

The cast of *Pobol y Cwm.* (BBC)

Prior to its establishment, Welsh-language programmes had been included on other channels, but the calls from activists for a dedicated Welsh channel reached their peak in 1980 when, with the Conservative Government backtracking on their promise of delivering a Welsh channel, Plaid Cymru president Gwynfor Evans threatened to go on hunger strike until it was settled.

Culturally, the channel provides extensive coverage of major Welsh events including the annual National Eisteddfod and Urdd Eisteddfod, and its most consistently watched programme, the long-running soap opera *Pobol y Cwm*.

Produced by BBC Cymru Wales where it was first broadcast in 1974 before switching to S4C and, fleetingly, to the rest of the UK on BBC 2, the series, set in the fictional Gwendraeth Valley village of Cwmderi, is filmed onset at Roath Lock in Cardiff Bay.

Welsh-language television scored a global hit in 2013 when it entered the world of crime noir with *Y Gwyll* (The Dusk, renamed Hinterland in English), a gritty crime drama set in Aberystwyth starring Richard Harrington as DCI Tom Mathias. Produced by Fiction Factory in partnership with Tinopolis, S4C and All3Media International, the series is filmed twice, with a Welsh-language version broadcast on S4C, followed by a bilingual version on the BBC to English-speaking audiences.

EARLY STARS OF THE SMALL SCREEN

In the 1960s, Port Talbot's **Bernard Fox** became a regular on two of America's biggest sitcoms, as Dr Bombay in *Bewitched* and as Colonel Crittendon in *Hogan's Heroes*.

Back home, memorable appearances from Welsh actors on national television during the 1970s include **Nerys Hughes** in *The Liver Birds*, **Gareth Thomas** as Roj Blake in sci-fi series *Blake's 7*, and possibly the most memorable cameo made by any Welsh actor, **Philip Madoc** as the U-boat captain in *Dad's Army*.

His wife at the time, **Ruth Madoc** from Pontypridd, would go on to find long-running success as Gladys Pugh in 1980s Bafta-winning sitcom *Hi-de-Hi!*, along with later appearances in shows such as *Little Britain* and *Benidorm*.

Another Welsh actor who established himself in a leading sitcom was **Windsor Davies** as Battery Sergeant Major Williams in *It Ain't Half Hot Mum*. Born to Welsh parents in Essex who relocated back to their native Nantymoel in Bridgend, the series also led to Davies scoring an unlikely number one single when, along with co-star Don Estelle, their cover of *Whispering Grass*, sung in character, topped the charts for three weeks in 1975.

Dame Siân Phillips from Gwaun-Cae-Gurwen, Neath Port Talbot, won the best actress award at the 1976 Bafta Awards for playing Livia Drusillain in the series *I, Claudius*, and was also nominated for *How Green Was My Valley* in the same year. Having made her film debut alongside Richard Burton and her husband at the time Peter O'Toole in *Becket* (1964), the Bafta connection continues to this day, with Bafta Cymru annually presenting the Tlws Siân Phillips Award to those who make a significant contribution to the industry.

In 2002, screenwriter Andrew Davies, best known for his adaptations of classics including *War & Peace* (2016), was made a BAFTA Fellow.

REGENERATING DOCTOR WHO

In 2005, when Swansea's **Russell T. Davies** (Stephen Russell Davies, b. 27 April 1963) set about regenerating the *Doctor Who* franchise in Wales following a sixteen-year hiatus, nobody could have imagined just how popular it would prove to be.

In his five-year tenure as executive producer, Davies, who had previously worked on *Queer as Folk* and Swansea-based *Mine All Mine*, oversaw as Christopher Eccleston took control of the Tardis and battled the Daleks in the first series, before successor David Tennant took things to even greater heights, topping the ratings charts and being shown in over fifty countries.

The fiftieth anniversary of *Doctor Who* in 2013. (BBC)

The success would lead to Davies producing two spin-off series, also based and made in Wales. *Torchwood* (2006) saw Doctor Who regular John Barrowman lead Welsh actors Eve Myles, Gareth David-Lloyd and Kai Owen as a group of extra-terrestrial investigators, while CBBC's *The Sarah Jane Adventures* (2007) allowed Elisabeth Sladen to reprise her role as the Doctor's companion from the 1970s. Davies also co-created *Wizards vs Aliens* in 2012 for CBBC.

Neath's **Julie Gardner**, then head of drama for BBC Wales who first approached Davies for the role, has since established the Bad Wolf production company with Jane Tranter which has bases in both Wales and Los Angeles, while production designer **Edward Thomas** from Swansea has been instrumental in putting Wales on the map as a filming location, bringing a considerable amount of work to the country, most notably at his hometown's Bay Studios where American series *Da Vinci's Demons* was filmed, and where he established YJB Films with Mal Pope.

For those looking to set off on a *Doctor Who* pilgrimage, the series is based in Cardiff Bay's Roath Lock, and many of its filming locations are situated in and around the city, with guided bus and walking tours available. Other locations can be found across Wales, with notable sites including Southerndown Beach in the Ogmore Vale and Margam Castle in Port Talbot, while the interactive Doctor Who Experience opened its doors in Cardiff Bay in 2011.

OH, WHAT'S OCCURRING?

When it comes to Welsh comedy on TV, it doesn't get much bigger than BBC Wales' commission of Baby Cow Productions' *Gavin and Stacey*.

A cult hit on BBC Three before switching to BBC One where it created stars of the principal cast and saw their catchphrases enter everyday conversation, the first episode in 2007 was watched by 543,000 people – the final episode on New Year's Day 2010 was seen by 10,250,000 people.

Split between Gavin's home in Essex and Stacey's family in Barry, **Joanna Page, Ruth Jones, Rob Brydon, Melanie Walters, Margaret John** and **Steffan Rhodri** flew the flag for Wales alongside the English contingent of **Mathew Horne, James Corden, Alison Steadman** and **Larry Lamb**.

In 2012, co-creator and writer Ruth Jones from Bridgend struck gold again with her follow-up Welsh sitcom *Stella* for Sky 1, produced by her Tidy Productions company with husband David Peet in which she also starred alongside **Craig Gallivan, Justin Davies, Steve Speirs, Patrick Baladi** and **Di Botcher**.

GAME OF THRONES AND
THE AGE OF THE BOX SET

The surge in big-budget television series in the early twenty-first century has seen British – and with it, Welsh – talent take on some of the biggest roles on American television, with **Michael Sheen** starring as Dr William in Showtime drama *Masters of Sex*, and **Matthew Rhys** as Philip Jennings in FX's Cold War series *The Americans*.

Welsh actors in the world-conquering gritty fantasy series *Game of Thrones* include leading roles for **Iwan Rheon** as the sadistic Ramsay Bolton, **Owen Teale** as Alliser Thorne, the Master of Arms at Castle Black, **Jonathan Pryce** as religious zealot the High Sparrow, **Robert Pugh** as Craster of the Free Folk, and **Margaret John** as Old Nan.

Other roles of note on American television shows include Olivier and Tony Award-winning actor **Roger Rees** from Aberystwyth, who established himself Stateside as Robin Colcord in *Cheers* and later as Lord John Marbury in *The West Wing*; Swansea-raised actor **Joseph Morgan** as Niklaus Mikaelson in *The Vampire Diaries*; and Amlwch's **Andy Whitfield,** who took the lead in *Spartacus: Blood and Sand* until his untimely death in 2011.

Iwan Rheon in National Theatre Wales' *The Devil Inside Him.*
(Toby Farrow / National Theatre Wales)

American series that have been filmed in Wales include *Da Vinci's Demons*, David S. Goyer's dramatisation of the life of Leonardo Da Vinci which was based in Swansea's Bay Studios, and Kurt Sutter's FX series *The Bastard Executioner*, set in the fourteenth century following Madog ap Llywelyn's rebellion and filmed in Cardiff's Pinewood Studio Wales.

COMEDY

Along with the rest of the UK, Wales embraced the variety stars that emerged from the music halls to find national and international fame on the radio and television in the twentieth century.

Gladys Morgan (1898–1983) was dubbed the 'Queen of Laughter' for good reason, because even if you couldn't remember her jokes, there was no way you could forget her riotous laugh, or her permanent, toothless grin. The diminutive Morgan – 4ft 10in tall – from Swansea adopted a broad Lancashire accent for her act, but reverted to her native twang when the opportunity to appear on BBC radio variety show *Welsh Rarebit* came about. She proved such a hit that she was retained as a resident on the show alongside Harry Secombe.

Stan Stennett (1925–2013) from Pencoed, Bridgend, gave his first impromptu performances during his time serving as an army bus driver in the Second World War, where he was able to fine-tune his jazz guitar and stand-up skills. A regular on *Welsh Rarebit* and *The Black and White Minstrel Show*, Stennett took up residency in Porthcawl's Grand Pavilion during the 1970s with one of his more popular creations, Billy and Bonzo the cross-eyed dog, and is fondly remembered for his stint in ITV soap opera *Crossroads* as Sid Hooper in the 1970s.

Alongside long-time comedy partner Mel Smith, **Griff Rhys Jones** (b. 1953) became the face of early 1980s alternative comedy, with the pair teaming up with Rowan Atkinson and Pamela Stephenson for the satirical sketch show *Not the Nine O'Clock News* (1979), and later in their own comedy vehicle, *Alias Smith and Jones* (1984), and the films *Morons from Outer Space* (1985) and *Wilt* (1989).

Rhys Jones was born in Cardiff but moved to West Sussex before his first birthday, and this theme of being an out-of-place Welshman would later form the basis of his book *Insufficiently Welsh* and television series *A Great Welsh Adventure* (2014). As a presenter, his shows have included BBC's *Bookworm* and the *Three Men in a Boat* series, as well as several Welsh-themed documentaries from his Cardiff-based production company Modern Television. Rhys Jones has won the Laurence Olivier Theatre Award for Best Comedy Performance twice, in 1984 for *Charley's Aunt* and a decade later for *An Absolute Turkey*.

Paul Whitehouse (b. 1958) also found himself at the forefront of the alternative comedy scene, and has since become one of Wales's most recognisable comic actors, described by American actor Johnny Depp as 'the greatest actor of all time'.

Born in Stanleytown, Rhondda Valley, before relocating to Enfield at the age of 4, it was while working as a tradesman with flatmate Charlie Higson on a house shared by budding young comedians Stephen Fry and Hugh Laurie that the pair were convinced to give comedy a go. Working closely with Harry Enfield, Whitehouse created two of his more memorable characters, Kebab shop owner Stavros and Cockney plasterer Loadsamoney, and appeared in sketches such as Smashy and Nicey and the Old Gits. Along with Higgins, he created *The Fast Show* in 1994, with his many characters including the Brilliant Kid and Unlucky Alf.

The popularity of BBC sitcom *Gavin and Stacey* has been credited with giving Welsh comedy a new impetus in the early twenty-first century, with a growth in popularity of localised comedy clubs, collectives and public platforms, and the likes of **Rhod Gilbert, Greg Davies, Elis James** and **Lloyd Langford** achieving success on stage, screen and radio.

Other comedians born in Wales include BBC's *Opportunity Knocks* winner **Mike Doyle** and *Absolutely Fabulous*' **Helen Lederer** from Carmarthenshire, *Have I Got News For You* mainstay **Ian Hislop** from Mumbles, **Dawn French** from Holyhead, while **Eddie Izzard** grew up in Skewen. Writer and performer **Peter Baynham** from Cardiff is a long-term collaborator with the likes of Steve Coogan, Sacha Baron Cohen, Chris Morris and Stewart Lee, co-writing the films *Borat* and *Alan Partridge: Alpha Papa*.

Wales has also played its own part in shaping some of its neighbour's biggest comedy stars. Iconic double act **Morecambe and Wise** first performed onstage together at Swansea's Empire Theatre in 1946; *Carry On* mainstay **Kenneth Williams** believed he was of Welsh decent; **David Mitchell** describes himself as being a quarter Welsh; London-born American superstar **Bob Hope** was born to a Welsh mother, as was Canadian funnyman **Leslie Nielsen**; and slapstick funnyman **Lee Evans** identifies with his Welsh roots through his father from Rhyl.

THE ULTIMATE WELSH DOUBLE ACT

Carmarthenshire duo Ryan Davies (22 January 1937 – 22 April 1977) from Glanamman and Ronald 'Ronnie' Williams (29 March 1939 – 28 December 1997) from Cefneithin found national fame in the 1960s when their Welsh-language comedy series *Ryan a Ronnie* proved to be so popular that it made the rare switch from Welsh into English to reach a wider audience.

When *Ryan and Ronnie* was launched across the UK, the pair – labelled the 'Welsh Morecombe and Wise' – brushed off accusations of selling out to record the show in London, and became the first comedians to make a series in both languages, which ran on BBC1 from 1971 to 1973.

Along with their sketches, in which Ryan played the fool to Ronnie's straight man, it featured music and special guests, including an appearance from Ken Dodd, and the popular Our House segment, a mock Valleys soap opera in which Davies, clad in a headscarf, played Mam, and Williams played the long-suffering Dad.

The pair spilt up in 1975 following their final performance at Caerphilly's Double Diamond Club, with Williams' ill-health cited as the reason. Diagnosed with severe depression, Williams all but disappeared from the public eye afterwards, making occasional reappearances in later life, including a role in *Twin Town* (1997), before taking his own life on Cardigan Bridge in the year of the film's release.

Ryan Davies during panto season at Swansea Grand
Theatre, 1976. (*South Wales Evening Post*)

Davies, who made his professional debut at the 1966 National Eisteddfod and met Williams while working in broadcasting, continued to work extensively – some would say over-worked – after the split, and established himself as one of the country's biggest stars. A successful musician, his album *Ryan at the Rank* (1975), which contains his trademark song, a hauntingly beautiful rendition of Joseph Parry's *Myfanwy*, was an instant bestseller.

He appeared alongside Richard Burton in 1972's *Under Milk Wood*, with Max Boyce in Harri Webb's satirical comedy *How Green Was My Father* (1976), and immortalised himself in Swansea Grand Theatre pantomime folklore, having first performed there with Williams in 1972's *Cinderella*, and continued until his sudden death from an asthma attack at the age of 40 in 1977.

Davies' son Arwyn followed in his father's Welsh television footsteps by joining the cast of soap opera *Pobol y Cwm* as long-running character Mark Jones in 1993.

JUST LIKE THAT!

The most famous Welshman to wear a fez, Thomas 'Tommy' Frederick Cooper (19 March 1921 – 15 April 1984), with his towering figure, ever-present cigar, and stuttering West Country – not Welsh – accent, was one of Wales' most successful and recognisable comedians.

Born in Caerphilly before moving to Exeter at the age of 3, magic was always his first love, having been introduced to the art at the age of 8 by his aunt. And despite the public perception that his tricks often failed, a technique he developed after realising that they received more laughs than the successful ones, Cooper was an accomplished magician and a member of the celebrated Magic Circle.

It was during the Second World War while serving in Egypt that his act first developed. As a member of the entertainment party, it was while performing a sketch that required a pith helmet that he borrowed a fez from a waiter – and the laughter it received made it a staple of his act.

A hardworking variety star, television propelled Cooper to superstardom, from his BBC debut in 1948 to his 1970s' heyday. But alcoholism would prove to be the entertainer's downfall, and in one infamous incident he very nearly killed talk show host Michael Parkinson in a guillotine act by forgetting to put the safety catch on.

Cooper died as he had lived, onstage, to rapturous laughter, after suffering a heart attack during *Live from Her Majesty's* in front of an applauding audience who believed it all to be a part of the act.

THE WELSH GOON

The anarchic, surreal, satirical radio show *The Goon Show* revolutionised comedy in the 1950s, and alongside Peter Sellers and Spike Milligan was Swansea's own Sir Harry Donald Secombe (8 September 1921 – 11 April 2001).

Born and raised in the St Thomas area of the city, Secombe's religious upbringing soon saw him singing in the church choir, a talent that he would combine with a flair for comedy after befriending Milligan while serving in Naples during the Second World War.

The story of their first encounter could itself have been a script from a Goon's sketch. Milligan's unit had somehow allowed a heavy artillery weapon to roll off a cliff, at the bottom of which was Secombe, sitting in his truck. Following the deafening crash of the howitzer landing, Secombe recalls that, 'the flap of the truck was pushed open and a young, helmeted idiot asked "Anybody see a gun?" It was Milligan.' To which he replied: 'What colour was it?'

Back home, Secombe was introduced to Sellers, and along with Milligan the trio were soon on the circuit, with Sellers crediting Secombe's singing voice for saving them on many an occasion. If the jokes fell flat, he could always resort to a tune.

In 1951, *The Goon Show* – then *Those Crazy People* – was commissioned, and it wasn't long before Secombe was picking up acting and musical roles. In 1963 he released what would become his trademark song, *If I Ruled the World* from Pickwick, and by the end of the decade he was hosting his own TV show, *The Harry Secombe Show* (1968). In later life he would turn his attention to religious programmes *Songs of Praise* and *Highway*.

When Secombe was knighted in 1981, he jokingly referred to himself as Sir Cumference due to his rotund figure. But two years later, his 19½ stone weight ceased to be a laughing matter when, warned by a doctor that he would die unless immediate action was taken, he rapidly shed the pounds – only to release his own diet book afterwards.

SOMETHING COMPLETELY DIFFERENT ...

As a founding member of the surreal comedy group Monty Python's Flying Circus, Terence Graham Parry 'Terry' Jones' (b. 1 February 1942) place in comic history is assured.

Born in Colwyn Bay, at the age of 14 Jones' family relocated to Surrey, and it was at Oxford University that he and his classmate Michael Palin began performing comedy.

They would collaborate together on television, radio and lyric writing, and it was their work on children's series *Do Not Adjust Your Set* with Eric Idle which is said to have caught the attentions of John Cleese and Graham Chapman, and soon after the legendary collective were formed.

Jones is described by the other members of the sketch show as the heart of the group, and was instrumental in ensuring that they pushed the boundaries of comedy. Jones and Palin's contributions are considered to be more abstract in nature, and his more memorable moments usually involved being dressed as a middle-aged woman.

Behind the camera, he would direct many of the Python's big screen outings, including *Monty Python's The Life of Brian*, the controversial religious feature length film which was met with resistance in many cinemas, remaining banned in Swansea until 1997, and which includes his most quoted line: 'He's not the Messiah, he's a very naughty boy!'

SMALL MAN IN A BOX

As a member of Porthcawl Comprehensive School's youth theatre group, a young Robert Brydon (Jones) (b. 3 May 1965) from Baglan, Port Talbot, met a young Ruth Jones, who would later offer him one of his defining roles, Bryn West in *Gavin and Stacey*.

Working for BBC Radio Wales from the age of 20, Brydon's television breakthrough came in 2000 with two BBC comedy series, *Human Remains* and *Marion and Geoff*, with the later spinning off into its own spoof chat show, *The Keith Barret Show* (2004).

Robert Brydon. (*South Wales Evening Post* / John Myers)

The start of a successful partnership with Steve Coogan, whose Baby Cow Productions produced both series, the pair appeared as fictionalised versions of themselves in Michael Winterbottom's *A Cock and Bull Story* (2005), which sowed the idea for *The Trip* (2010) and *The Trip to Italy* (2014). The sitcom is notable not only for the performances of the pair, which must rank as some of the best in their careers, but from a Welsh perspective, for the free rein given to Brydon to discuss his hometown, Port Talbot, and impressions of its three main actors – Richard Burton, Anthony Hopkins and Michael Sheen – all featuring prominently in the improvised script.

In 2009, Brydon and Jones reprised their roles from *Gavin and Stacey* and, accompanied by Tom Jones and Robin Gibb, reached the top of the charts with the Comic Relief charity single *(Barry) Islands in the Stream*. Brydon became the host of comedy panel show *Would I Lie to You?* in the same year, and has been a regular guest and chairman on BBC Radio 4's *I'm Sorry I Haven't a Clue* since his first appearance in 2006.

THE BIRTH OF FILM

Film making began in Wales at the end of the nineteenth century, with the earliest known recording being American cinematographer Birt Acres' short documentary *Prince and Princess of Wales Arriving in State at the Cardiff Exhibition*, filmed during a royal visit in 1896.

Two years later, English-born Arthur Cheetham became the first Wales-based filmmaker, shooting silent films of local interest in Rhyl, starting with *Children Playing on the Beach at Rhyl* (1898). William Haggar soon followed suit in the south, with 1903 chase film *Desperate Poaching Affray* considered an influential forerunner of the genre.

During the First World War, Henry Edwards directed and starred alongside Florence Turner in *A Welsh Singer* (1915), a love story based on Allen Raine's novel of a shepherd and his young love who becomes an opera star, while the Welsh Prime Minister who led the country during the war became the subject of what is believed to be the first full-length biopic of a political figure. *The Life Story of David Lloyd George* was filmed in 1918, but controversy surrounding the filmmaker's alleged unpatriotic reasons for making the film saw solicitors representing Lloyd George, who had originally backed the production, buying the only copy and suppressing it from view. The film didn't get its first public showing until 1996.

THE GOLDEN AGE

The Golden Age of Hollywood is said to have started in 1927 – the year when Wales' largest theatrical talent, Ivor Novello, took to the screen in Alfred Hitchcock's early films *The Lodger* and *Downhill*.

E.E. Clive from Blaenavon established himself as a prolific minor-role-playing actor in the 1930s, making his debut in *The Invisible Man* (1933). But the Hollywood dream turned sour for Port Talbot-born stage actress Peg Entwistle in one of the more tragic tales in Welsh film history, who symbolically committed suicide by throwing herself from the giant 'H' on the Hollywood sign in 1932 – a month before the opening of her debut film, *Thirteen Women*.

In the 1930s, Hollywood came to Wales when Boris Karloff visited to star in the first Hollywood talking film to be shot in the country, James Whale's comedy horror *The Old Dark House* (1932). It was followed by *The Citadel* in 1938, directed by legendary Hollywood director King Vidor and based on A.J. Cronin's novel in which a Scottish doctor arrives in the village of Blaenely to treat the miners suffering from tuberculosis. It was nominated for four Academy Awards.

During the Second World War, *The Silent Village* (1943) was a timely piece of propaganda produced by the government-run Crown Film Unit and directed by Humphrey Jennings. The documentary-style short film recreated the massacre at the Czechoslovakian mining village of Lidice in South Wales, and served as a reminder of what might have happened had the German invasion succeeded.

In the same year, Barry-born actor Roger Livesey appeared in the first of three successful films from Powell and Pressburger, *The Life and Death of Colonel Blimp* (1943).

THE MINER ON SCREEN

The Proud Valley (1940) was one of the first films to portray the harsh realities of life down the mine, in which David Goliath, an African American who arrives in the fictional South Wales village of Blaendy, takes up a job as a miner and sings in the male voice choir.

Directed by Pen Tennyson and starring American actor Paul Robeson, a political activist who developed a close affinity with the Welsh working classes, it was filmed predominantly in Ealing Studios with some scenes shot on location in Neath and the Rhondda Valley, and became the first film to be premiered on radio when the BBC Home Service broadcast an edited version.

A year later, John Ford's *How Green Was My Valley* (1941), based on Richard Llewellyn's novel of a community adapting to the changing way of life around the coalfield, took the Welsh miners to the world with a film that won five Academy Awards, beating *Citizen Kane* to the Best Picture award, and was nominated for five more.

But while the film might be based in Wales, the Second World War meant that it was filmed in black and white in Malibu Creek State Park, California, rather than in colour in Wales as intended, and the Welsh accents of many of the actors sound suspiciously Irish. In fact, the film only has one Welsh actor, Rhys Williams from Swansea, who was himself only hired to teach the other actors how to speak with a Welsh accent, but ended up landing the role of supporting character Dai Bando.

Socialist filmmaker Jill Craigie explored nationalisation in the Welsh coal industry in drama *Blue Scar* (1949), which was named after the blue-coloured scar left by the coal dust. Starring Emrys Jones and Gwyneth Vaughan with a score from Grace Williams, it was filmed in a studio assembled in Port Talbot's unused Electric Theatre, with scenes also shot in Abergwynfi.

Matthew Warchus' *Pride* (2011), based on the true story of the bond formed between the London gay and lesbian community and the striking miners of Onllwyn in Neath in the early 1980s, is one of the warmest portrayals of a Welsh mining community on film – with some impressive Welsh accents from Bill Nighy and Imelda Staunton.

WALES' FIRST OSCAR-WINNING ACTOR

In 1946, Neath-born actor Ray Milland (3 January 1907 – 10 March 1986) beat off competition from the likes of Bing Crosby and Gene Kelly to become the first Welsh actor to win the Academy Award for Best Actor for his portrayal of alcoholic writer Don Birnam in *The Lost Weekend* (1945), which also claimed the Best Picture award.

Having relocated to America following the success of *The Flying Scotsman* (1929), Milland – born Alfred Reginald Jones, but taking his surname from the Mill Land area of his hometown – starred alongside some of the biggest names in Hollywood, including John Wayne in

Reap the Wild Wind (1942) and Grace Kelly in Alfred Hitchcock's *Dial M for Murder* (1954) and *To Catch a Thief* (1955).

In a career which spanned eight decades, the versatile Milland turned his attention to directing and television in the 1950s, often directing himself in his own films, and along with his reputation as a handsome leading man, is also defined by his cult films in the developing horror and sci-fi genres, including *The Premature Burial* (1962) and *X: The Man with the X-Ray Eyes* (1963).

FILM IN THE SECOND HALF OF THE TWENTIETH CENTURY

Richard Burton, arguably Wales' greatest actor, made his film debut in 1949's *The Last Days of Dolwyn* alongside his friend and the film's writer and co-director Emlyn Williams. Williams had been active in the film industry since 1932's *The Frightened Lady*, but this was the only film he directed, alongside Russell Lloyd, which tells the fictional tale of an all-too-real scenario in which a Welsh village is due to be flooded to supply water to Liverpool.

Richard Burton and Elizabeth Taylor in Port Talbot. (*South Wales Evening Post*)

In the same year, Donald Houston from Tonypandy, Rhondda Cynon Taf, filmed his two biggest Hollywood films, *The Blue Lagoon* (1949) and *A Run for Your Money* (1949), and would later appear alongside Burton in *The Longest Day* (1962) and *Where Eagles Dare* (1968).

With the release of Biblical epic *Ben-Hur* in 1959, Wales found itself back at the Oscars, with Hugh Griffith from Marian-glas, Anglesey, claiming Best Supporting Actor for the role of Sheik Ilderim. Griffith would again be nominated for the same award in 1963 for *Tom Jones*.

Crime drama *Tiger Bay* (1959), starring Sir John Mills and his daughter Hayley, was shot mainly on location in Cardiff and Newport, and offers a tantalising glimpse into Cardiff Bay at the time, with faithful depictions of the area's docks, pubs and street culture.

Llanelli-born actress Rachel Roberts was propelled to stardom in the early 1960s playing an older mistress in two provocative films, *Saturday Night and Sunday Morning* (1960) and *This Sporting Life* (1963), which saw her nominated for the Academy Award for Best Actress.

In 1962, Peter Sellers comedy *Only Two Can Play* was filmed and set in Swansea (renamed Aberdarcy), based on Sir Kingsley Amis' novel *That Uncertain Feeling*, which he'd written in the city while lecturing at Swansea University.

During the 1960s, Monmouth-born poet, comedian and actor Victor Spinetti firmly established himself as a companion of the Fab Four by appearing in three Beatles films, *A Hard Day's Night* (1964), *Help!* (1965) and *Magical Mystery Tour* (1967).

In 1971, entertainer Tessie O'Shea from Cardiff, a musical star who regularly headlined the London Palladium and shared the top billing in the Ed Sullivan show with The Beatles, made the biggest film appearance of her career alongside Angela Lansbury in musical fantasy *Bedknobs and Broomsticks*.

Karl Francis from Bedwas, Caerphilly, who began his career as a television producer, took on the role of writer and director in 1977 for his seminal documentary drama *Above us the Earth*. The story of the closure of Ogilvie Colliery in the Rhymney Valley uses a mixture of professional and amateur actors, along with news footage gathered from the time, and remains a powerful social commentary of the period.

1978 saw the arrival of the country's most-loved and most-quoted sports film, the comedy *Grand Slam*. Written by Gwenlyn Parry and John Hefin, it starred Hugh Griffith, Windsor Davies, Dewi 'Pws' Morris and Sion Probert as a group of rugby-mad Welshmen who head to Paris to watch Wales take on France in the Five Nations Championship.

In the 1980s, director Peter Greenaway, who was born in Newport and became famed for his stylised, artistic films, started and ended the decade with two of his best known works, *The Draughtsman's Contract* (1982) and *The Cook, the Thief, His Wife & Her Lover* (1989), while Cardiff-born director Andrew Grieve adapted Bruce Chatwin's novel *On the Black Hill* (1987), a drama set and filmed in the Welsh border which spans eighty years in the lives of Welsh twins.

MEN OF HARLECH

Sir Stanley Baker (28 February 1928 – 28 June 1976) from Ferndale, Rhondda Cynon Taf, established himself on the silver screen in such seafaring films as *Captain Horatio Hornblower R.N.* (1951) and *The Cruel Sea* (1953), before making his first of many Hollywood appearances in *Knights of the Round Table* (1953).

His first leading role arrived in Cy Endfield's *Hell Drivers* (1957), and the pair formed a successful partnership, going on to make six films together including one of the most iconic depictions of the Welsh on screen – 1964's *Zulu*, in which he both starred and produced.

As the final assault looms in the epic showdown between the British Army and the Zulus at the Battle of Rorke's Drift, hundreds of Zulu warriors sing their war chant as they prepare to attack. With narration from Richard Burton, the Welsh troops, led by Ivor Emmanuel, respond in a rousing rendition of male voice choir favourite 'Men of Harlech', spurring on the severely outnumbered troops.

THE PORT TALBOT THREE

For whatever reason – a gritty working-class ambition, the prominence of superior youth theatre groups, or simply something special in the water – the industrial steel town of Port Talbot has proven to be a conveyor belt of Welsh talent, and has produced three of the country's biggest success stories.

Richard Burton (Richard Walter Jenkins, 10 November 1925 –
5 August 1984) from Pontrhydyfen remains the benchmark for Welsh
actors; a phenomenal talent who became one of the highest-paid actors
in the world and burned bright while wrestling with his alcoholism
which would, ultimately, drive him to an early grave at the age of 58.

The son of a coal miner who took the surname Burton after being
adopted by his former teacher Philip Burton, his natural affinity at
school was towards sport, and he was quoted in later life as saying
that 'I would rather have played for Wales at Cardiff Arms Park than
Hamlet at the Old Vic.'

But having had a taste of acting in a Port Talbot youth drama
group, he quickly established himself as a renowned Shakespearian
actor, before emerging through the ranks of British film to make his
Hollywood debut in *My Cousin Rachel* (1952), for which he won the
Golden Globe Award for New Star of the Year.

Burton was also nominated for an Academy Award for the film
but missed out, a pattern that would repeat itself throughout his life.
Denied that elusive Oscar on seven occasions, Burton was also shortlisted for *The Robe* (1954), *Becket* (1964), *The Spy Who Came in from
the Cold* (1965), *Who's Afraid of Virginia Woolf?* (1966), *Anne of the
Thousand Days* (1969) and *Equus* (1977).

Burton was married five times and had four children, but it was his
two successive marriages to Elizabeth Taylor – with whom he'd started
an affair while filming the financially bloated historical epic *Cleopatra*
(1963) – that fuelled the tabloids with their headline-grabbing stories
of excessive wealth and public quarrelling.

A proud Welshman to the end, Burton was laid to rest near his home
in Céligny, Switzerland – allegedly for tax reasons, despite his personal
wishes to be buried back in Port Talbot – in a Welsh red suit and with
a copy of the *Complete Works of Dylan Thomas*.

There are parallels that can be drawn between the lives and careers of
Burton and Margam-born actor **Sir (Philip) Anthony Hopkins** (b. 31
December 1937).

Both learnt their trade in Port Talbot, excelled in the works of
Shakespeare, and went on to conquer Hollywood, but where their
paths differ is that Hopkins was triumphant in his battle with
alcoholism – and was awarded an Oscar at the first time of asking.

Having made his stage debut in Swansea Little Theatre's 1960
production of *Have a Cigarette* at Swansea's Palace Theatre, he was
soon spotted by Laurence Olivier who offered him a place at the Royal
National Theatre. Opportunities on screen soon followed, with early

Sir Anthony Hopkins in Port Talbot YMCA, 2008.
(*South Wales Evening Post* / Gayle Marsh)

roles including Richard I in *The Lion in Winter* (1968) and David
Lloyd George in *Young Winston* (1972), before taking larger parts in
The Elephant Man (1980) and *The Bounty* (1984).

But it was his spine-chilling take on serial killer Hannibal Lector
in *The Silence of the Lambs* (1991) that propelled Hopkins to
superstardom, sweeping the boards at most awards ceremonies and
claiming nine awards for best actor. Hopkins would reprise the role in
two sequels, *Hannibal* (2001) and *Red Dragon* (2002).

Musical in his youth, Hopkins returned to composing in later life,
and saw his waltz *And the Waltz Goes On*, originally written at the
age of 19, performed by André Rieu in 2011. The following year he
released *Composer*, an album of classical compositions which included
a piece entitled *Margam*.

Unlike Burton and Hopkins, **Michael Christopher Sheen** (b.
5 February 1969), who has established himself as one of Wales' most
versatile performers, was born in Newport, but was raised in Baglan
when his parents returned to their hometown.

At the age of 12, Sheen showed promise as a footballer and was
offered a place in Arsenal's youth team, but his parents – both of whom
were involved in the stage, with father Meyrick earning a side-line as a
Jack Nicholson look-alike – decided against moving to London, and it
was acting that won out.

Sheen began performing with the highly acclaimed West Glamorgan Youth Theatre, a group still close to his heart who he continues to champion, before performing with the National Youth Theatre of Wales and studying at London's Royal Academy of Dramatic Art, making his West End debut in *When She Danced* at The Globe Theatre in 1991.

Excelling on stage during the 1990s in London and abroad, his performances in *Amadeus* (1998) and *Look Back in Anger* (1999) were both nominated for Olivier Awards. On screen, Sheen took his first leading role in 2002's *Heartlands*, and in 2003 was directed by Stephen Fry, who he had previously appeared alongside in 1997's *Wilde*, in his adaptation of Evelyn Waugh's *Vile Bodies*, *Bright Young Things* (2003).

In the same year, he made his first appearance as the recurring protagonist Lucien the werewolf in the *Underworld* films, before making the part of then-Prime Minister Tony Blair his own in *The Deal*, a role which he later returned to in the Academy Award-winning drama *The Queen* (2006) and *The Special Relationship* (2010).

A biopic specialist, Sheen memorably portrayed Kenneth Williams in *Kenneth Williams: Fantabulosa!* (2006) and Brian Clough in *The Damned United* (2009), and having starred as David Frost in the London and Broadway production of Peter Morgan's *Frost/Nixon*, reprised his role for the big screen Academy Award-nominated *Frost/Nixon* (2008).

THE WELSH QUEEN OF HOLLYWOOD

When Catherine Zeta-Jones (b. 25 September 1969) chanted oggy, oggy, oggy, oi oi oi! as she accepted her Best Supporting Actress award at the British Oscars for *Chicago* in 2003, and later thanked everyone back home in Swansea as she claimed her Academy Award for the same role, it was proof, if proof were needed, that you can take the girl out of Wales, but you can't Wales out of the girl.

Having made her stage debut as the lead in *Annie* at Swansea Grand Theatre, Zeta-Jones' television breakthrough arrived in 1991 alongside David Jason in *The Darling Buds of May*, before landing her first big screen film role – thanks to the recommendation of Steven Spielberg, who had spotted her in television miniseries *Titanic* (1996) – in Martin Campbell's *The Mask of Zorro* (1998) with Anthony Hopkins and Antonio Banderas.

In the same year, she met Michael Douglas at Deauville Film Festival, and two years later the pair would marry at New York's Plaza Hotel, with a reception which included a shipment of Brains beer, a Welsh choir, and a wedding ring made from Welsh gold from Aberystwyth.

Catherine Zeta-Jones at the 2010 Ryder Cup Welcome to Wales concert
at Cardiff's Millennium Stadium. (*South Wales Evening Post*)

In 2010, Zeta-Jones returned to the stage in Sondheim's *A Little Night Music*, and claimed the Tony Award for Best Actress in a Musical for her Broadway debut.

MODERN-DAY WALES AND THE MOVIES

The 1990s would prove to be a defining decade for film in Wales, with the Welsh division of the British Academy of Film and Television Arts, Bafta Cymru, launching its own red carpet award ceremony in 1991, and a new breed of actors and directors all coming to the fore.

Rhys Ifans (b. 1967) from Haverfordwest, a regular face on Welsh-language television, made his film debut in *Twin Town* (1997), which paved the way to a show-stealing supporting role in *Notting Hill* (1999). Other films have included *Harry Potter and the Deathly Hallows – Part 1* (2010) and *The Amazing Spider-Man* (2012).

Ioan Gruffudd (b. 1973) from the village of Llwydcoed, Rhondda Cynon Taf, also cut his teeth on S4C, notably as a long-running cast member of *Pobol y Cwm*, before establishing himself on the big screen in 1997 in *Wilde* and James Cameron's blockbuster *Titanic*.

Matthew Rhys (b. 1974) from Cardiff – Gruffudd's former housemate and best man at his wedding – took his first major role playing Dylan Thomas in *The Edge of Love* (2008), with earlier films including *Titus* (1999) with Anthony Hopkins and *Very Annie Mary* (2001) with Jonathan Pryce.

Behind the camera, Cardiff-born director **Marc Evans** (b. 1963) claimed the Bafta Cymru award for Best Director for *House of America* in 1997, a gritty drama set in a down-on-its-luck Welsh mining community starring Siân Phillips and Matthew Rhys. Evans, who would go on to direct *My Little Eye* (2002),

Mal Pope, Gwenllian Hughes, Marc Evans and Edward Thomas at the Leicester Square premiere of *Jack to a King*, 2014.

Trauma (2004), and *Snow Cake* (2006), reunited with Rhys in 2010 for *Patagonia*, a drama about the Welsh settlement in Argentina which also featured the director's wife Nia Roberts and singer Duffy.

In Swansea, Evans directed 2011's *Hunky Dory*, the tale of a teacher trying to stage a rock musical version of Shakespeare's *Tempest*. It starred Minnie Driver, whose father was born in the city. 2014's *Jack to a King – The Swansea Story* turned its attentions to the city's football team. Produced by YJB Films, the rags to riches documentary charts the real-life story of Swansea City AFC's dramatic rise from the foot of the football league to the heights of the Barclays Premier League.

In 1997, Swansea-born director **Kevin Allen** (b. 1959), whose acting roles include appearances in alternative comedy series *The Comic Strip Presents* and Danny Boyle's *Trainspotting* (1996), directed anarchic black comedy *Twin Town*, which has itself been dubbed 'The Welsh Trainspotting' .

Co-written with Paul Durden, it was set and shot in his home town and neighbouring Port Talbot, and starred real-life brothers Llŷr and Rhys Ifans as the Lewis twins in an unromanticised account of life in Swansea at the time, complete with drugs, crime and joyriding. It also included a cameo from the director's Llanelli-born brother **Keith Allen** (b.1953), the prolific actor, comedian, presenter and musician, and father of singer Lily Allen.

Popular Welsh coming of age films from the period include *Human Traffic* (1999), written and directed by **Justin Kerrigan** and set in the club scene of his native Cardiff; *Very Annie Mary* (2001), from Rhyl actress, writer and director **Sara Sugarman** starring Rachel Griffiths and Jonathan Pryce; and *Submarine* (2010), based on Swansea author **Joe Dunthorne**'s debut novel which marked the directorial debut of Richard Ayoade with original music from Arctic Monkeys frontman Alex Turner.

In 2011, director **Gareth Evans** from Hirwaun, Cynon Valley, having relocated to Indonesia, unleashed the martial arts action thriller *Raid: The Redemption*, while **Caradog W. James** brought sci-fi back to Welsh cinema in 2013 with *The Machine*.

Wales can also lay claim to having the world's smallest solar-powered movie theatre, the mobile Sol Cinema based in Swansea, while Gower Heritage Centre has Wales' smallest theatre, the twenty-three-seater La Charrette.

WELSH-LANGUAGE FILMS

In 1935, Urdd founder Ifan ab Owen Edwards' *Y Chwarelwr* (The Quarryman), which took a look at the life of a slate quarryman in Blaenau Ffestiniog, became the first Welsh-language talking film.

But until the arrival of S4C in 1982, Welsh-language films were few and far between, although HTV did try – if admirably fail – to dub three well-known English films into Welsh: *Frankenstein Must Be Destroyed*, *The Sin of Father Mouret* and *Shane*. Watching the likes of Peter Cushing and, more comically, Alan Ladd, speaking in Welsh was met with a predominantly negative reaction.

In 1986, *Rhosyn a Rhith* (Coming Up Roses), the tale of a South Wales community's fight to keep the local cinema open, became the first Welsh-language film to be released in London's West End.

The director and musician Endaf Emlyn (b. 1944) from Bangor was a leading figure in Welsh-language film in the 1990s. Following his first full-length feature for S4C, 1988's *Stormydd Awst* (Storms of August), he adapted Caradog Prichard's novel *Un Nos Ola Leuad* (One Moonlit Night) in 1991, while 1993's *Gadael Lenin* (Leaving Lenin), a comedy about a group of Welsh students and teachers who visit Russia, was voted the most popular British film at the London Film Festival.

1990s *Hedd Wyn*, an anti-war biopic based on the life of the Welsh poet killed in the First World War, became the first Welsh-language film to be nominated for an Oscar in the Academy Award for Best Foreign Language Film category.

In 1999, director Paul Morrison's *Solomon a Gaenor* (Solomon and Gaenor), a tragic love story starring Ioan Gruffudd and Nia Roberts, was also nominated for an Oscar, and *Eldra* (2002), Timothy Lyn's film of a Romani girl growing up in 1930s Bethesda, was chosen by Bafta to represent the UK but did not make the finals.

ANIMATION IN WALES

Wales endeared itself to generations of children with the stories of Ivor the Engine, a locomotive for The Merioneth and Llantisilly Rail Traction Company Limited who lived in the top left-hand corner of Wales with such wonderfully named friends as Jones the Steam and

Evans the Song. Launched in black and white in 1959, Ivor returned in full colour in 1975.

In 1983, S4C animated the adventures of SuperTed, based on the heroic teddy bear created by Mike Young in 1978. Already a popular series of books and a cuddly toy, the series was produced by Siriol Productions, who also brought Jennie Thomas and J.O. Williams' 1920s children's books Wil Cwac Cwac (Will Quack Quack) to the screen.

Sam Tân (Fireman Sam) followed in 1987, based on an idea dreamed up by two fire-fighters from Kent, which was developed by Young with illustrator Rob Lee. The residents of Pontypandy have now been broadcast in over forty countries.

English animator Joanna Quinn relocated to Wales in 1985 and established Beryl Productions with partner Les Mills, and has since received Academy Award nominations for *Famous Fred* (1996) and *The Wife of Bath* (1998).

In 2003, Y Mabinogi (known as Otherworld in English), an animated adaption of the graphic novel based on the ancient Welsh tales, featured music from John Cale with the voices of Matthew Rhys and Ioan Gruffudd.

WALES AND THE BIG MOVIE FRANCHISES

James Bond: Stanley Baker turned down the opportunity to become the first Welshman to play Ian Fleming's British Secret Service agent in 1961, unwilling to commit to a three-film contract. Possibly realising his mistake, he did later try – unsuccessfully – to land the role of a villain.

The accolade would instead go to Timothy Dalton from Colwyn Bay, Denbighshire, in *The Living Daylights* (1987) and *Licence to Kill* (1989). A long-time target for the producers, Dalton was first offered the role following the departure of Sean Connery, but considered himself too young at the time. A darker Bond than had gone previously, his portrayal was considered to be more faithful to Fleming's source material, if less appealing to those who had grown more accustomed to the suave and witty Bond portrayed on screen.

One of the mainstays of the Bond films is the invention of increasingly ingenious gadgets supplied by the Q Branch, and it was Desmond Llewelyn from Newport who made the role of Q his own. Making his first appearance in 1963, he continued until his death in 1999, appearing in seventeen films alongside five different Bonds.

Squaring off against Bond in *Tomorrow Never Dies* (1997) was Jonathan Pryce from Carmel, Flintshire, as media mogul Elliot Carver. The Olivier Award-winning actor, whose first major film role was in Terry Gilliam's *Brazil* (1985), also appeared in blockbusters *Evita* (1996) and *The Pirates of the Caribbean* (2003).

Penbryn Beach in Ceredigion doubled up as North Korea in *Die Another Day* (2002), but when the filmmakers requested to shoot scenes for *Spectre* (2015) in the capital's Senedd chamber at the National Assembly for Wales, their request was denied.

Wales's other significant contribution to the series has been supplying some of its more well-known theme tunes, with Shirley Bassey's *Goldfinger*, *Diamonds are Forever* and *Moonraker*, and Tom Jones' *Thunderball*.

Star Wars: In 1977, George Lucas launched the world's most iconic film franchise – and in 1979, Wales launched the world's most iconic space ship. When a life-sized Millennium Falcon, as flown by Han Solo in the space opera, was needed for 1980 sequel *The Empire Strikes Back*, it was assembled, 70ft in diameter and weighing 23 tonnes, in a top secret location in Pembroke Dock which now houses a permanent exhibition.

In 1983, it was a Welshman who took the reins of the climatic finale to the original trilogy when director Richard Marquand from Llanishen, Cardiff, landed the job of director on *Return of the Jedi*, having impressed Lucas with his 1981 spy film *Eye of the Needle*, based on the book by Cardiff-born best-selling author Ken Follett.

In 1985, Siân Phillips appeared in the made-for-TV movie *Ewoks: The Battle for Endor*, but of all the Welsh actors who have played minor roles in the franchise, the most memorable contribution came from Andy Secombe – the son of Harry Secombe – who supplied the voice for computer-generated junk store salesman Watto in the first two of the prequels, *The Phantom Menace* and *Attack of the Clones*.

Tolkien's Middle-earth: Wales had a significant influence on the books of J.R.R. Tolkien, who studied the culture, including the myths of the *Mabinogion*, and was known to have stayed in Talybont-on-Usk, Brecon Beacons, while writing parts of *The Lord of the Rings*.

Evidence can be found in the place names and languages used in his stories – it's no coincidence that the Elves sound Welsh when they speak – and specific real-life locations, such as the Buckland Estate on the River Usk, which is believed to have been the inspiration for the Buckland group of Hobbits.

Of all the Welsh actors to appear in Peter Jackson's big screen adaptions, the two biggest contributions came from John Rhys-Davies who played the dwarf Gimli, a primary character and a member of the Fellowship of the Ring who set out to defeat the Dark Lord Sauron in *The Lord of the Rings* trilogy, and Luke Evans as Bard the Bowman in *The Hobbit* trilogy.

Harry Potter: There are several Welsh references in J.K. Rowling's record-breaking seven-book series about the boy wizard and his time at Hogwarts, many of which carry over into the films.

Wales fields a national Quidditch team which competes in the World Cup, with two regional teams known to be the Caerphilly Catapults and the Holyhead Harpies. A national day of mourning was held in Wales when legendary Catapults player 'Dangerous' Dai Llewellyn was eaten by a Chimaera while on holiday in Greece.

The Welsh dragon makes an appearance, but instead of the traditional red, the country's native fire-breathing reptile is the Common Welsh Green, which appeared during the Triwizard Tournament in *Harry Potter and the Goblet of Fire*.

Hogwarts founder Professor Helga Hufflepuff is said to have been born in Wales during the tenth century and her portrait adorns a wall in the school, while Rowling has revealed that the Welsh 'Singing Sorceress' Celestina Warbeck was modelled on Shirley Bassey.

Welsh actors who appear in the eight films include Rhys Ifans as the eccentric Xenophilius Lovegood, Steffan Rhodri as Reginald Cattermole, Paul Whitehouse as the Welsh Knight of the Round Table Sir Cadogan, Shefali Chowdhur as Harry's Yule Ball date Parvati Patil, and Ryan Nelson as Ravenclaw student Michael Corner.

Freshwater West in Pembrokeshire, which also featured in Ridley Scott's *Robin Hood*, was the setting for the protagonist's Shell Cottage, as well as a pivotal scene featuring Dobby the house elf, in *Harry Potter and the Deathly Hallows – Part 1 and Part 2*.

Superheroes: Actor Christian Bale, who was born in Haverfordwest, became the first caped crusader born on Welsh soil when he donned the cowl in Christopher Nolan's *Batman Begins* (2005), while it was Richard Brake from Ystrad Mynach who shot down Bruce Wayne's parents as the criminal Joe Chill. The bat cave was also made in Wales, with the 88ft-high Henrhyd Falls waterfall in Brecon Beacons doubling up as his secret lair in *The Dark Knight Rises* (2012).

In the same year, Ioan Gruffudd led Marvel's superhero team the *Fantastic Four* as the elasticated Mister Fantastic. He would also voice DC's Mister Miracle in the *Justice League Unlimited* animated series.

When Marvel's god of thunder took to the big screen in *Thor* (2011), it was Anthony Hopkins who starred as his father Odin, and when Andrew Garfield found himself bitten by a radioactive spider in *The Amazing Spider-Man* (2012), it was another Welshman who would prove to be his biggest adversary, as Rhys Ifans turned green and scaly as the villainous Lizard.

On the small screen, Swansea's Matt Ryan brought DC Comics' chain-smoking anti-hero John Constantine to life in the NBC series *Constantine* (2014), while Penarth's Erin Richards plays James Gordon's fiancée Barbara Kean in *Gotham* (2014).

DYLAN THOMAS ON SCREEN

The voice – and words – of Dylan Thomas live on in the world of film.

Thomas himself wrote screenplays, including *The Three Weird Sisters* (1948) and *No Room at the Inn* (1948) with producer Ivan Foxwell, and short propaganda films for the Ministry of Information during the Second World War.

The only known film footage of Thomas emerged in 2014, with the poet seen fleetingly walking on the sands of Pendine as an extra in a crowd scene in Ava Gardner and James Mason film *Pandora and the Flying Dutchman* (1951).

His more famous poems are often referenced on screen, no more evident than the prominent role that 'Do not go gentle into that good night' played in Christopher Nolan's 2014 Academy Award-winning space epic *Interstellar*.

Richard Burton presented Jack Howells' Academy Award-winning short *Dylan* in 1963, the only Welsh film to win an Oscar. He later recorded *Under Milk Wood* in 1953, and again with wife Elizabeth Taylor and Peter O'Toole for the 1972 film adaption – the only film in which all three of them appeared together. Directed by Andrew Sinclair and shot predominantly in Wales, Burton's narration would also be posthumously used for an animated version in 1992.

Thomas' idealised vision of Christmas in Swansea, *A Child's Christmas in Wales*, has been a popular choice for stage, screen and radio. In 1987, Don McBrearty directed Denholm Elliott in a made-for-television take on the story.

In 1990, Anthony Hopkins directed Bob Kingdom in *Dylan Thomas: Return Journey*, a narration of short stories which was recorded and released on DVD and later revived for the stage in 2014.

It took forty-four years – the longest period in history between a screenplay being written and filmed according to the *Guinness Book of Film Facts and Feats* – for Thomas' *Rebecca's Daughters* to see the light of day. Having been written in 1944, the comedy in which a revolt is led against an over-taxing aristocracy was filmed in Cardiff's Hensol Castle in 1992 by director Karl Francis.

Wartime romance *The Edge of Love* (2008), which starred Matthew Rhys as Thomas in a complex love triangle with Vera Phillips (Keira Knightley) and Caitlin Thomas (Sienna Miller), was filmed across Wales, most notably in New Quay.

The 2014 centenary celebrations saw a flood of Thomas-themed productions, with BBC Cymru Wales assembling a who's who of famous Welsh faces for a narration of *Under Milk Wood*, which included Bryn Terfel as the Revd Eli Jenkins.

Kevin Allen directed a more visceral take on the play for voices. Initially released as the Welsh-language *Dan y Wenallt* (2014), it again featured a wealth of Welsh talent, including Rhys Ifans as Captain Cat and Charlotte Church as Polly Garter.

Two of the more memorable biographical representations of Thomas came courtesy of Tom Hollander and Anglesey's Celyn Jones, who both starred in Bafta Cymru award-winning films in 2014.

Hollander piled on the pounds to portray Thomas in his final days for *A Poet in New York*, filmed in Wales by Griff Rhys Jones' Modern Television, while Jones cut a riotous figure alongside Elijah Wood as Thomas' long-suffering American agent John M. Brinnin in director Andy Goddard's *Set Fire to the Stars*, also filmed in Wales and featuring a soundtrack from Gruff Rhys.

BIBLIOGRAPHY

Below a list of books that have, along with periodicals, encyclopaedias and websites, either been invaluable to my research or are recommended as further reading.

In particular, I would like to single out the works of Dr John Davies, whose books have been a constant source of inspiration not only for this book, but for my career as a whole. If anyone would like to read a *big* book of Welsh culture, I recommend *The Welsh Academy Encyclopaedia of Wales* (University of Wales Press, 2008), written by Davies with Nigel Jenkins, Menna Baines and Peredur I. Lynch.

Bell, David, *The Artist in Wales* (George G. Harrap & Co., 1957)
Bogdanov, Michael, *Theatre: The Director's Cue* (Capercaillie Books, 2013)
Borrow, George, *Wild Wales* (Collins, 1955)
Bragg, Melvyn, *Rich: The Life of Richard Burton* (Coronet, 1989)
Cone, John Frederick, *Adelina Patti: Queen of Hearts* (Scolar Press, 1993)
Davies, John, *Broadcasting and the BBC in Wales* (University of Wales Press, 1994)
Eric, Rowan, *Art in Wales 2000 BC – AD 1850* (University of Wales Press, 1978)
Fawkes, Richard, *Welsh National Opera* (Julia MacRae, 1986)
Holroyd, Michael, *Augustus John* (Pimlico, 2011)
Hughes, Owain Arwel, *My Life in Music* (University of Wales Press, 2012)
Jobbins, Siôn T., *The Welsh National Anthem* (Y Lolfa, 2013)
Jones, Dedwydd, *Black Book on the Welsh Theatre* (Bozo, 1985)
Lord, Peter, *Imaging the Nation* (University of Wales Press, 2004)
Lycett, Andrew, *Dylan Thomas: A New Life* (Weidenfeld & Nicolson, 2003)
Meredith, David and Smith, John, *Obsessed* (Gomer, 2012)
Owen, Trefor M., *Welsh Folk Customs* (Gomer, 1994)
Rees, Jasper, *Bred of Heaven* (Profile Books, 2012)
Roderick, A.J., *Wales Through the Ages* Vols 1 & 2 (Christopher Davies Ltd, 1965)
Sager, Peter, *Wales* (Pallas, 1991)
Stephens, Meic, *The Literary Pilgrim in Wales* (Gwasg Carreg Gwalch, 2000)
White, Eryn M., *The Welsh Bible* (Tempus, 2007)
Williams, J.E. Caerwyn, *The Poets of the Welsh Princess* (University of Wales Press, 1994)
Williams, Jeremiah, *Christopher Williams* (The Delyn Press, 1955)